PROPHETIC KEY

Book 7 - The Prophetic Field Guide Series

COLETTE TOACH

www.ami-bookshop.com

PROPHETIC KEY
Book 7 - The Prophetic Field Guide Series

ISBN-10: 1-62664-154-4
ISBN-13: 978-1-62664-154-9

Copyright © 2016 by Apostolic Movement International, LLC
All rights reserved
5663 Balboa Ave #416,
San Diego,
California 92111,
United States of America

1st Printing November 2016

Published by **Apostolic Movement International, LLC**
E-mail Address: admin@ami-bookshop.com
Web Address: www.ami-bookshop.com

All rights reserved under International Copyright Law.
Contents may not be reproduced in whole or in part in any form without the express written consent of the publisher.

Unless specified, all Scripture references taken from the New King James Version®. Copyright © 1982 by Thomas Nelson. Used by permission. All rights reserved.

Contents

Contents	3
Part 01 – Preparing for Prophetic Office	10
Chapter 01 – Transitioning to Prophetic Office	10
Who This is NOT For	12
The Anatomy of the Prophet Ready for Office	12
Ready for Office	18
Chapter 02 – What Qualifies You for Office	22
Understanding Authority	23
How You Qualify	25
When Your Training is Put on Hold	32
Chapter 03 – The Office Readiness Checklist	36
Key #1: Passing the Final Test	38
Key #2: Arrangement of Circumstances	45
Key #3: Positioning of Relationships	47
Chapter 04 – Defining the Prophetic Child	50
The Prophetic Child Defined	51
Preparation of the Prophetic Child	54
Chapter 05 – Raising a Prophetic Child	64
1. Get Over Yourself	65
2. Identify Their Abilities and Limitations	67
3. Lay a Foundation	71
4. Arm Them for Battle	74

- Chapter 06 – Prophetic Marriage: Husbands 80
  - Let's Get Real.. 83
  - Husbands, Love Your Wives 85
- Chapter 07 – Prophetic Marriage: Wives 94
  - The Submission Definition.. 94
  - God's Part 104
  - Something for the Singles 104
- Part 02 – The Authority of Prophetic Office 110
- Chapter 08 – Character of Prophetic Office 110
  - The Character of Prophetic Office........................... 112
  - Be Prepared to Let Go 119
- Chapter 09 – The Prophet in the Local Church........... 122
  - Ministry vs. Office 124
- Chapter 10 – Navigating The Local Church Rules 136
  - Rule #1 Administrative Order................................... 136
  - Rule #2 Meeting Order.. 140
  - Rule #3 Find the Right Approach............................. 142
- Chapter 11 – The Prophet in the Universal Church..... 150
  - The Universal Church Personality 152
  - Your Transition to the Universal Church 154
- Chapter 12 – The Prophetic Key................................... 164
  - Prophetic Ministry vs. Prophetic Office................... 168
  - Functions of the Prophetic Key 172
  - Stop Talking and Start Doing 177

- Chapter 13 – Prophetic Authority 182
  - The Origination of Authority 182
  - Defining Authority 184
  - Summary 204
- Chapter 14 – Prophetic Rejection 208
  - The Ugly Duckling 209
  - Incorrect Ways to Respond to Rejection 212
- Chapter 15 – Making Rejection Work for You 220
  - Making Rejection Work for You 226
  - Step 3: Do not Defend Yourself 230
  - Conclusion 233
  - Vindication is at Hand 233
- Part 03 – Practical Prophetic Office 238
- Chapter 16 – Becoming the Image of Christ 238
  - From Stones to Boulders 238
  - Conformed to His Likeness 242
  - Passion for Jesus 254
- Chapter 17 – Resurrection: Becoming a Rock 258
  - Give Him Your Heart 258
  - The Secret Place 260
  - Small Beginnings 264
  - How to Minister to Jesus 265
  - Going Through the Process 268
- Chapter 18 – Increasing the Prophetic Anointing 272

    Prophetic Anointing Reminder 273
    How to Release the Anointing 276
    You Know the Motto: Always Be Prepared! 282
    Changing Power 285
Chapter 19 – Becoming a Prophetic Minister 288
    The 12 Step Program 289
Chapter 20 – Prophetic Counseling: Inner Healing 316
    The Pastoral Prophet 318
    The Five Step Counseling Process 322
    This is Real Ministry 335
Chapter 21 – Appointment to Prophetic Office 338
    The Necessity of Laying on of Hands 339
    Making the Transition 341
    The Gentle Breeze of Jesus 343
    Hear His Word for You Right Now 344
END NOTE – Where to From Here? 346
About the Author 349
Recommendations by the Author 351
    Prophetic Mandate 351
    Prophetic Essentials 352
    Prophetic Functions 352
    Prophetic Anointing 353
    Prophetic Boot Camp 353
    Prophetic Warrior 354

Prophetic Counter Insurgence 354
A.M.I. Prophetic School 355
Contact Information 356

PART 01 – PREPARING FOR PROPHETIC OFFICE

CHAPTER 01

TRANSITIONING TO PROPHETIC OFFICE

Part 01 – Preparing for Prophetic Office

Chapter 01 – Transitioning to Prophetic Office

The more you learn, the more you realize how little you really know. It is at this stage of the journey that your prophetic ministry comes into focus. It was as if you were looking through a frosted glass pane, trying to reach for the impossible.

However, the closer you have gotten to your goal of prophetic office, the more unprepared you feel to walk it out. There was a time when all you wanted to be was a prophet. There was a time when "prophetic office" was all that consumed your thoughts and intention.

As you have engaged in spiritual warfare, faced the truth of your flesh in training, and have racked up your "frequent flyer miles" to your visits to the cross, a new revelation begins to dawn on you. You are not ready.

There is still so much to learn. There is still so much flesh to be crucified. No matter how proficient you have become with your sword, you are painfully aware of the weaknesses in your offense and the gaps in your armor.

> **KEY PRINCIPLE**
>
> It takes a prophet who has been on the way a little while to have eyes so keenly trained that they can see the flaws in themselves.

What sets one warrior apart from the other is not just skill. It is a willingness to improve and the humility to pick out any weakness that would give the enemy an advantage on the battlefield.

And so as we plunge headlong into the subject of prophetic office and the final book of *The Prophetic Field Guide Series*, you have been on a long journey with me.

You have been equipped. You have gained knowledge and have come to understand your journey. Your flesh has been challenged and you have learned more about what a prophet is not, to reveal in you everything a prophet is.

With each step that you have taken, the Holy Spirit has stripped a veil from your eyes and replaced it with a piece of armor. The more you have been stripped and then equipped, a new revelation has begun to form. It is only when you "get it" that the chapters to follow will make any sense for you.

Who This is NOT For

This book is not for you if you just recently got a conviction of your prophetic call. Please go to *Prophetic Essentials* and work your way through!

This book is not for you if all you want is to "reach prophetic office." By now you should realize that being a prophet is a lot more than just having a position.

This book is not for you, if you have not learned to "die already" and willingly submit your flesh to the cross.

This book is not for you if you have not yet learned the essentials of prophetic warfare and learned how to use your spiritual weapons.

This book is not for you if you have not gone through any form of prophetic training.

Why? Why the hard line so early on in this book?

It is because I plan to take you by the hand and transition you from prophetic ministry to office. This is a vital part of your progress, but a complete waste of time if you are not ready for that transition!

The Anatomy of the Prophet Ready for Office

Do you remember how long it took the Holy Spirit just to get you to the place of acknowledging your call? Well this is another one of those turning points in your life and it is not a roulette wheel where you get to "hit or miss" it.

This is not a lucky guess or a desperate hope that you can "quickly get prophetic office" without going through the process.

In fact, if you have not gone through the process already, you will not make this transition at all.

So with that being said, allow me to illustrate for you what someone ready for this book looks like.

ONCE UPON A TIME...

You finally received a conviction of your call, only for everything to be turned upside down. Instead of doors opening, they seemed to shut in your face. Ministry opportunities closed down and the Lord began to draw you aside.

This was frustrating for you at times. You knew you were called to be a prophet. You knew you were meant to deliver His word, but instead of being released, you were shut down instead. You wanted to move forward! You wanted to rise up as a prophet, but people either used you because you could hear from God, or they did not acknowledge your prophetic call at all.

... THERE WAS CHERITH

And so your journey began. Your frustrations led you into the presence of Jesus where you finally felt the shelter you so desperately needed. His words were honey to your lips and oil to your broken soul. It was in the secret place that you came to know Him face-to-face and to realize that this journey of yours always had a purpose.

Those closed doors had a purpose. At the end of that season though, you did not care what the purpose was any longer. You lost the world and gained Christ. As you allowed Him to lead you into the quiet, you finally became content with your place.

Enter: Zarephath

In this first transition (from Cherith to Zarephath), you were still not ready. There was so much more that God needed to do with you! Just as you came to peace with being the outcast and going to Jesus alone, the stripping truly began.

Hurts from the past, your flesh, and your bitterness started being triggered from every side. The church, family, workplace and friendships… it did not seem to matter which way you turned, because each time you did, a rejection was waiting to sideswipe you.

It took you a while to "get it." It took you a while to realize that it was not what everyone was doing to you that mattered, but how you responded. It was not the rejection that mattered as much as the fact that you always reacted in bitterness.

Step by step, the Lord required more of you. He required your bitterness, anger, and guilt. He required your bad habits and sin. Once you had surrendered all of those, the digging got even deeper.

He began to require your righteousness. You were even stripped of the spiritual things that were your boast. The gifts of the Spirit sometimes just dried up as if He was trying to make a point. He was reminding you over and over again, that you had been called by His grace and not your own good works.

The stripping was intense, but it did not leave you naked. In fact, He began to arm you with both knowledge and wisdom - enough knowledge and wisdom to engage in spiritual warfare. Once you realized that more often than not, you were your own worst enemy, the Holy Spirit began to teach you something else!

You discovered how much the enemy had been using your own failure and sin as a weapon against you! You learned that you were set free by the cross and that you no longer had to take it!

Just as your confidence began to grow, that was around the time you mistook the voice of the enemy for the Lord, and ended up with a mouthful of mud as you fell flat on your face, once again.

CARMEL WAS NEXT – YOUR ACHILLES HEEL

This was the turning point for you. It was one thing to succeed, but how did you handle failure? What was the one thing that the Holy Spirit tried to have you deal with again and again?

Was it your rebellion? Was it stubbornness? Was it an inability to submit or take correction from others? Perhaps your "Achilles heel" was that you never followed through with anything in your life.

The final test came, and this weakness was displayed before you in Technicolor surround sound. There was no avoiding it.

The final battleground of your final test was not what you expected and in that moment, you warred within yourself. Should I choose the spirit or should I choose the flesh? Should I defend myself, or should I remain silent as Jesus remained silent when facing judgment from man?

What you might not have realized is that in that moment, you made a decision that would forever change your life and lead you down a road that has led you to this very point. It is not just the fact that you faced a test that you qualify for prophetic office.

It is rather the nature of the test that brings you to the point of readiness for the chapters that follow.

Making the Transition

You see, that test you faced did more than prove to the Lord that you qualify for the final round.

> **KEY PRINCIPLE**
>
> It has proven to you that your calling does not depend on your ability to excel. Your calling depends on your ability to surrender.

When given a choice to do things God's way or your way, you chose God's way. When chosen to respond in the flesh or the spirit, you surrendered to the spirit (amidst much travail!)

When given the choice to run away or to keep facing the cross, you faced the cross. When given the choice to justify yourself or to take the blows – you offered the other cheek.

This is somebody who is ready to wield the prophetic key.

Now perhaps you have wondered why the tests you have faced up until this point had been so intense. The Lord knows your heart. He knows that you will do anything for Him and that you love Him with all of your soul!

So why this intensity? Why does the Lord find it so necessary to press His point so strongly? Why the trip down "deception lane"?

Well there is nothing quite as humbling as falling into deception as a prophet to remind you that you are not here by a choice of your own will.

You see, you need to know that! You need to realize as you stand ready today, that you do not stand here by your own will. You did not call yourself. You did not arm yourself. You did not train yourself.

Your flesh did not perfect the spirit!

READY FOR OFFICE

You stand here today by the grace and power of God. Your ability will always have limitation, but His continues with the expansion of the universe.

His power is immeasurable! If you lean on yourself, for just a moment, you will find yourself lacking. If for just a moment you think that your office was achieved because of your own tenacity or personality power, it will not take much for the devil to convince you that you made it all up.

However, when you come to a conviction of realizing that you did nothing to merit this call, but to simply be chosen of God, you can trust Him to finish what He started as well.

When God picks you up and uses you when you know very well that you just failed, it blows your mind. All along, you thought that if you could just remain holy, that He would use you more, yet He decides to use you in your greatest moments of weakness.

Now that is God. That is a calling! When all is said and done, do you finally realize why you stand ready for the next step in your calling?

It is because of this...

> ***1 Corinthians 1:27*** *But God has chosen the foolish things of the world to put to shame the wise, and God has chosen the weak things of the world to put to shame the things which are mighty;*
> *28 and the base things of the world and the things which are despised God has chosen, and the things which are not, to bring to nothing the things that are,*
> *29 that no flesh should glory in His presence.*
> *30 But of Him you are in Christ Jesus, who became for us wisdom from God - and righteousness and sanctification and redemption -*
> *31 that, as it is written, "He who glories, let him glory in the Lord.".*

CHAPTER 02

WHAT QUALIFIES YOU FOR OFFICE

Chapter 02 – What Qualifies You for Office

You can always see a new recruit to the army - white lines around their neck where they just recently had their hair cut short, ruddy faced and sure that they can conquer the world.

They think that they know what boot camp entails and imagine that "they will be just fine." They think that they can handle anything that is thrown at them.

It does not take long though for them to reel under the pressure and the continual change that is expected of them. It is no different from the prophet who is first called to the ranks in God's army.

When the call first comes, you are ruddy faced and excited to take on this new challenge. You imagine days of beating up the devil, giving profound prophetic words, and changing the Church with a single prophecy.

Then reality hits. Training begins and you realize that before you can change the Church, the change must originate from your own life. Your prophetic words, which were once so sought after, are soon rejected and you wonder what it is you did wrong.

You know how it goes. As you submit to the training, you become fitter. Your spiritual legs become stronger and soon the ruddy faced recruit is replaced by an officer who is ready to take up their position.

Everyone knows that a commander is not made overnight. He rises up through the ranks and he stands up to command others because of the price he was willing to pay in his own life.

UNDERSTANDING AUTHORITY

So what is it that sets a commander apart from a new recruit? Other than the obvious fitness level, it is something quite beyond skill or even desire.

What makes the troops obey a commander and not that little private (who might even have a better idea)? The answer is quite simple... authority!

This is something we sadly misunderstand in the Church. We mistake "skill" for authority. We mistake anointing for authority, however these two are quite different. Consider these passages.

> ***2 Corinthians 13:10*** *Therefore I write these things being absent, lest being present I should use sharpness, according to the authority which the Lord has given me for edification, and not for destruction.*

So what has all this training been for? To make you into a better prophet? No, you do not yet understand. This process has been for a single purpose – to qualify you to carry the authority of the prophet.

Here is where we begin to separate prophetic ministry from prophetic office. Up until now you have functioned in prophetic ministry. You have learned how to hear the voice of God.

You have learned how to prophesy and walk in the spirit. You have learned how to do spiritual warfare. In fact, I would daresay that you have undergone quite the transformation over the last couple of months.

You have shed the flesh and gained the Spirit of God. You have become more keen to the sound of the spirit, and you can spot a demon if it tries to sneak past you. With all of this knowledge and ability though, you are still not in prophetic office.

How so? Well consider this natural illustration. If a private in the army shoots and runs better than all his companions, does this automatically make him their commander?

Just because a new recruit is highly skilled at something, does this give him the right to order the others around and wear a new uniform? Hardly. His attempts might make others notice him, but it is only when he is given that promotion that he will carry that authority.

Until that time comes, it is quite possible that the very skilled recruit will have to submit to a very harsh and (possibly) very unskilled Sergeant Major!

Can you see why this has lead the Church astray? As a believer receives their call and begins to move in the gifts of the Spirit, this skill is recognized, mistakenly, as authority.

Any believer can flow in the gifts of the Spirit. Any believer has the potential to hear from God. So if everyone can do it, what is left for the prophet to do? Well by now, you should know exactly what all is involved.

How You Qualify

In fact, through the last six books in the series, I have outlined your training and your job. You are just lacking one more thing, and I promise, that missing piece is not more anointing!

That missing piece is what I like to call, the prophetic key. The authority to root and to plant. It is the kind of authority that seals a person into a position whereby they are granted a piece of God's authority, just like it tells us in Romans 13:1.

Now apostle Paul understood that authority. When he tells us of the work he is doing in 2 Corinthians 13:10, he makes sure that we know that he is doing it, *"according to the authority which the Lord has given me…"*

He might have been a great teacher, but his teaching skill is not what he placed his boast or position on. He proved his place by the authority that was given to him directly from the Lord.

So how can you "earn" that authority? Well the first thing you should have realized by now, is that no amount of righteousness or begging will get it.

There is no amount of works or holiness that will help you qualify for it. In fact, I would daresay that there is a single principle that ensures your placement of authority and it lies in this single word… obedience!

> *Acts 5:32* *And we are His witnesses to these things, and so also is the Holy Spirit whom God has given to those who obey Him.*

I am not going to just mention this and then leave you hanging. I have entire chapters on the subject of the prophetic key and prophetic authority.

OBEDIENCE

There is one reason why you are standing on the cusp of prophetic office today, and I promise, it is not because you got it right. I do not need to tell you that though, because as you stand looking over this unknown land spread before you, you see your flaws.

You see your inability and you compare it to the grace that the Lord is about to give you. You tremble, realizing that your flesh is capable of so many nasty things. You feel the potential pride inside of you.

You sense your fear and even some guilt from failures of the past. If you were to put all of that on a balance, your shortcomings would undoubtedly win out every time.

Thank the Lord for His grace. Thank goodness that He chose you because of what He can do and not because of what you can do. Thank the Lord that He is able to finish in you what He began.

You need not start in the spirit and end in the flesh. Rather you can just let the Holy Spirit finish the work now and take you by the hand as you step over this final threshold and allow Him to put the weight of the authority on your shoulders.

It is obedience that opened the door in the first place remember? The Lord called and you obeyed. The Lord told you to give up family, friends and church... and you obeyed.

The Lord asked you to give up worldly things and you put away the television, burned old books and deleted things that had no place on your computer. The Lord challenged your love and although you had no more to give, you obeyed and gave the bit you had.

What you do not realize is that with each process you have gone through, it was always obedience that took you a step forward and it is obedience that will take you up another level again.

Like I already said, it is your obedience that has qualified you to move forward with each phase of your training. The reason why this is so powerful is what obedience has helped shape in you.

You now have the anatomy of a prophet! As you have submitted to the hand of the Holy Spirit on the potter's wheel, you have not only proven your loyalty, but you have been keenly shaped to become the exact vessel to do the job He needs you to do.

> **KEY PRINCIPLE**
>
> Your part was to obey. His part was to shape you. The more you obeyed, the more He shaped you.

Now you can never stand up and say to everyone, "I am self-made!" because you know the truth.

You know that every last etching in your soul and brush stroke of color was made by the Holy Spirit. Your only boast is that you did not move from the potter's wheel. He was the real artist, and you? Well you were just a shapeless piece of clay until He got going.

Funny how we all start out thinking that our misshapen piece of clay is "the bomb," only to realize as we mature, how messed up we really are!

You look now at the new recruits around you, and you smile on one hand and cringe on the other. They are so bold and confident in what they think they have to offer God. They come with their long list of credentials and you see how much that stands in the way of their true potential.

No worries though. If their calling is genuine, they will go through the same process you did, and before long, they will be looking on the newbies with the same understanding of maturity that you now have.

There is nothing quite like having gone through boot camp and have engaged in the prophetic battlefield to knock you down a few notches, is there?

So now, you do not qualify because you can speak in diverse tongues and minister to more people than anyone else. If that was the case, the leaders we would see in the church would all be brilliant and above reproach... but they are not, are they? No, they were just obedient in the thing that God told them to do.

Their obedience opened doors just like it did for the New Testament saints. Jesus told them to "go forth." They "went forth." They started a movement that we are still riding today. Simple really.

To fulfill that mandate though, the Lord had to bring about some change. He had to add a few key players, but because the Church had been obedient, the ground was prepared for that change.

Is the ground of the Church prepared for the change to come? Well it is going to take your obedience to bring her to this point, so we must move forward, because we have a lot of work to do.

CONTINUAL CHANGE

Obedience alone does not qualify you for office. Also, being obedient just once does not cut it either. A recruit is not going to make it to officer status if he works really hard one day and then goes AWOL the next! He has to be consistent and push through no matter what, if nothing else, just to stand in the ranks!

It is the same with you. A single obedience is not what is going to get you to office. So you obeyed the Lord and followed His call, but then you did not want to give up your bitterness. The first obedience does not overrule the next. Why? It is because your continual obedience is essential for continual change.

Do you remember this passage?

> ***2 Corinthians 3:18*** *But we all, with unveiled face, beholding as in a mirror the glory of the Lord, are being transformed into the same image from glory to glory, just as by the Spirit of the Lord.*

> **KEY PRINCIPLE**
>
> As you continue to look at the Lord, you are continually changed. It is this change, along with your obedience that qualifies you.

No one is appointed to officer status until they have gone through the full training process and qualified! The same holds true for you.

So often the prophet-in-training wants to skip to the end and just be placed! I have seen this so many times mentoring prophets. I had one student who was really going through the throes of training. She barely hit the *Prophetic Warrior* phase, and decided that she was further along than we would admit and wanted to go directly to the teachings on prophetic office.

She could identify with some of the training and deemed that she had enough qualities now to "cut it." Unfortunately, though, she did not see the process through. There were some things that were not in line yet – her marriage, for example! Her husband was unsaved and nowhere ready to give her the kind of support she would need.

Instead of obeying God and allowing Him to bring this final change to her circumstance, she jumped the gun. Back to the wilderness she went.

CHANGE OF CIRCUMSTANCES

It is exciting to see God change you through the *Prophetic Boot Camp* phase. You begin to flow in the gifts as never before. You hear the Lord Jesus so clearly and you are swept into the beauty of His presence.

You become keener in the spirit, discerning what is the enemy and what is the Lord. It is in this moment you might be tempted to think that you are ready for the final phase.

Now it could well be that you are spiritually ready for prophetic office – but are your circumstances and the people around you ready?

This is why obedience is essential. It is not just for the purpose of shaping you, but for preparing the Church as well!

Moses might have thought he was ready to bring deliverance – but the people sure were not! It took them time, and it will take your circumstances and spouse time as well. The Lord is well aware of that.

WHEN YOUR TRAINING IS PUT ON HOLD

I consider my own journey and how often the Lord held me back so that Craig could be put in place as well, so that we could walk together.

I have had the Lord put a prophet's spiritual training on hold to do nothing else, but invest into their marriage for a long season. Why? Because it is going to take a lot more than just you being ready to unleash you on the Church!

Your circumstances and the people in your life need to be in the right position as well! Are you unmarried? Has it occurred to you that the Lord has your training on hold, because He wants to bring you a spouse first so that you can grow together and be equally yoked?

You should realize by now that achieving prophetic office is not for your benefit. Do generals and commanders exist because the military wanted to make a nice place for gifted individuals?

No! These positions were instituted for the benefit of the nation. If the man in that position does not qualify, it is a nation that suffers. It is those under them that pay the price.

So do not think that prophetic office was made for you.

> **KEY PRINCIPLE**
>
> Prophetic office was made for the Church, and both you and the Church need to be ready for that.

It depends on where the Lord wants to send you. Is there a local church that He wants to send you to? Is there a particular ministry or vision that He needs you to accomplish?

Well before you reach prophetic office, there are some things that need to be taken into account first.

Firstly, have you been obedient? Are you exactly where the Lord needs you to be right now?

Secondly, have you stayed on the potter's wheel and completed the full cycle of change that the Lord wanted to bring about in you, in spirit, soul, and body?

Thirdly, are your circumstances in line to allow you to take your place once you are placed?

Finally, are your relationships in line and can they accommodate this office? Is your marriage and family in order? Will these relationships assist your call or destroy it from the inside?

You are about to learn exactly what kind of doors need to open and what you need to do to fulfill your prophetic office, so before you run headlong into it, make sure that everything is in line and that you are ready for it!

So let me bring all four of those points together for you, so that you can gauge for yourself exactly how ready you are for prophetic office.

1. Obedience
2. Transformation
3. Arranged Circumstances
4. Complimenting Relationships

Now, short of working on relationships and being obedient, what can you do right now to ensure that you reach prophetic office? Yes, we know that the Holy Spirit is the only one that can do the work. He is the only one that can shape you.

But surely, there has to be something that you can do right now to help the process along. Fortunately, there is! So let's take a quick look at what you can do to take these final steps towards prophetic office.

CHAPTER 03

THE OFFICE READINESS CHECKLIST

Chapter 03 – The Office Readiness Checklist

It was hard to convince my second daughter, Jessica, that she was well able to let the Lord use her in writing. She had a rough start in her reading career. It took us a long time to realize that she needed glasses. Add to that a good dose of dyslexia and it left a "limp" in her emotionally.

Now I knew she was capable of being amazing. Convincing her of that however, took a bit more time. The Lord began to put pressure on her and brought her to a place where she simply did not have a choice.

She was appointed as the Bookshop manager for our ministry and part of the job description was to send out a weekly encouragement to all the customers. I will not forget the first encouragement she had to write.

It took her hours to try and put one together – only for it to fail terribly and she had to write it again. She wanted to run away, but had no choice but to press through.

I knew she could do it. The Lord knew she could do it. The entire team knew she could do it. She, however, was not convinced that she could do it and this is what took the longest time of all.

While she did not realize her hidden potential, everything she tried to write came out wrong. Eventually she came to the end of herself and received a fresh conviction from the Lord. Skill or no skill... she was going to do this unto the Lord.

Well, as they say, the rest is history! From the moment the "penny dropped," she began writing with a newfound skill and charisma. It is the same with your calling.

> **KEY PRINCIPLE**
>
> The Lord knows what you are both capable and incapable of. He knows the weakness of your flesh and the strength of your spirit. The problem is, you do not know it yet!

Do you think that the Lord needs to see whether or not you will pass a test? He knows the end from the beginning! He knows very well what you are capable of. What the training process does give you is a revelation... of yourself!

He is about to give you the kind of authority that can tear up someone's life if you do it wrong. He is about to bestow on you, the kind of power that if you should fall for satan's tricks, can be used against the kingdom of God instead of for it!

So you better know if you have a problem with bitterness. You better be pretty sure that you do not take kindly to correction or know how to obey! Above all, you need to know that you have inside of you a dispensation of grace that will enable you to overcome that flesh when the Lord needs you to the most!

So the key to reaching prophetic office is not just about your righteousness or how well you pass the tests. There is a bit more involved that you need to take into consideration here.

All of us are familiar with a combination lock. It is the kind that can only be opened if you enter the correct digits. If not... that lock remains shut tight. Well when it comes to prophetic office, there is a certain combination that you need to enter office.

Well for the rest of this chapter, I am going to give you the combination to unlock that chain! It will encourage you to see what God has done and also what you can expect Him to do very soon in your life!

Key #1: Passing the Final Test

So what is your thorn in the flesh?

That is probably the one thing that the Lord has been putting His finger on time and again. Go over the last nine months and what is the one death or process that still leaves a nasty sting when you think back on it?

If you feel the sting... you are not over it yet! You have not yet overcome and as a result, you are not aware of your limitations or abilities as a prophet. You do not know the capability of your flesh, so how then will you qualify to expose the flesh of others?

> **2 Corinthians 12:7** *And lest I should be exalted above measure through the abundance of the revelations, there was given to me a thorn in the flesh, the messenger of Satan to buffet me, lest I should be exalted above measure. (KJV)*

What is the thing that keeps tripping you up? You see, this test is two-fold. Firstly, it exposes the thorn in you. Secondly, it gives you the opportunity to overcome that thorn using the grace of God and not your own abilities.

Perhaps by now you have realized that you cannot overcome the flesh, with the flesh! Well that is why you need this test. To expose your thorn so that the enemy can never use it against you or the Church again.

Now my thorn was the inability to submit. I was happy to give my life for anyone... as long as it was not unfairly demanded of me. I would have considered myself quite the "giver" until, of course, I was demanded to give. Well, then I really did not want to give any longer!

I wanted to be in charge of the giving here. It was my life to be poured out. It was my emotions and will that were to be offered as a gift and as far as I was concerned, it was up to me to decide when, where, and to whom to give all of that to.

Well like I said, I thought I was quite the giver until I was taken advantage of. I was happy to work hard and invest my life until someone started making demands on me that I thought were unfair.

As things turned out, I was not quite the giver I thought I was. I gave to receive. I gave to get acceptance. I gave to get love. The problem with all of this? I gave… to *get*.

But then the Word of God tells me,

> **Matthew 5:39** *But I tell you not to resist an evil person. But whoever slaps you on your right cheek, turn the other to him also.*
> *40 If anyone wants to sue you and take away your tunic, let him have your cloak also.*
> *41 And whoever compels you to go one mile, go with him two.*

"Are you kidding me Lord? I just gave everything I had to this person and they slapped me in the face… and you want me to do it again?!"

"Yes."

"Yes?! YES?! Are you wanting me to suffer here? You see how much they are hurting me. Don't you care?"

"Yes I care. Now love as I love."

I was not impressed. I felt like a victim and I felt like the whole world was just taking a piece of me. My husband needed me, my kids needed me, work needed me, family needed me. Everyone wanted and wanted and there was nothing left of me… for me.

Well it turns out that it is exactly what God wanted from me. He had called me to be poured out as an offering to His people and how could I be poured out when I still tried to control when I was willing to be spilled?

You see, the Lord wanted to be the giver. He just needed me to be obedient. He did not need my precious moral code or self-righteousness. He just needed my obedience and this test taught me a lot about myself.

Firstly, I realized that I was not quite the giver I thought I was. In fact, I was downright selfish. I liked having things my way. I had this notion that the way I thought was the right way of thinking and everyone in the world should think that way!

I did not like to be told what to do and I felt insecure under someone else's leadership. Turns out, that on top of not being a giver, I had some serious trust issues as well.

How could I boast a trust in the Lord, if I could not trust those He delegated authority to over me?

Here I stood, wanting to change the Church and root out every evil in it when I did not even have the basics of love and faith left when I was put through the fire.

> **KEY PRINCIPLE**
>
> Nothing quite like having your "gold" melted away in the fire to realize that all that glistened… was just plain dross!

I put in a truckload of what I thought to be gold, and got back a nugget of the pure stuff. The rest? Well that was just fluff and dross. The rest was my big mouth shouting out all my great intentions and ideas – none of which God really needed.

Thank the Lord for miracles though. Because who would have guessed… He could create something incredible from such a tiny nugget of gold!

In fact, that is all that the Lord needed. He did not need anything but my obedience – and He worked miracles with it!

OPEN YOUR EYES

> *John 9:39 And Jesus said, "For judgment I have come into this world, that those who do not see may see, and that those who see may be made blind."*
> *40 Then some of the Pharisees who were with Him heard these words, and said to Him, "Are we blind also?"*
> *41 Jesus said to them, "If you were blind, you would have no sin; but now you say, 'We see.' Therefore your sin remains.*

There is never a more ridiculous statement than, "I am so humble." Because everything in it screams the complete opposite. No one that is humble says that they are humble!

No one that truly has love, boasts in their love, and no one that is righteous boasts in their righteousness!

It is because you walk in righteousness that you see the darkness in your heart. It is because you love so much that you understand how fragile your emotions are and how quickly they can turn on you.

> **KEY PRINCIPLE**
>
> It is when you are humble that you consider yourself so very, very far from true humility!

This kind of revelation only comes from passing that final test. To allow the Lord to open your eyes to the things that truly drive you.

It is only when you allow the light of the Lord to shine into your heart that you allow Him to illuminate the dark places that you have hidden from yourself and the rest of the world.

In this moment, you will see your pride and self-righteousness. The thing is, you will only see it, if you let the light shine.

The test will arrange circumstances and the kind of pressure that will bring your darkness up into the light. Now you have a choice to make.

You can either see the darkness in yourself for what it is, or you can choose to point out the darkness in others in the hope that their black heart will somehow justify and cover yours.

What purpose does this serve? You are meant to be a prophet! You are called to a life of death and personal sacrifice! You are called to be a model to the Church. So should your love not be covering their sin?

Instead, you try to cover your sin with their sin... and you wonder why you have not yet qualified for prophetic office?

Has God disqualified you because you have sin? No! Go back to John 9:49! It is because you *say* you have no sin, that your sin remains.

It is because you say that you have no sin, that you are disqualified. There is something powerful about seeing your sin for what it really is. It enables you to cover it over... not with more sin... but with the blood!

In that moment, you will understand why you qualify as a prophet. It is because, through your obedience, you allowed the grace of God to lead you and His blood to cover your sin.

If you can continue to walk in that, you qualify.

> **KEY PRINCIPLE**
>
> You qualify to carry His authority not because you are perfect, but because you know the perfection of Christ.

KEY #2: ARRANGEMENT OF CIRCUMSTANCES

We have spoken long and hard about the training you will go through as a prophet, but one thing we have not looked at is what it is going to take for your ministry to get moving. You will learn, as you reach prophetic office, that a drastic shift will take place in your circumstances.

I find it an incredible tapestry of miraculous design when the Lord places one of His prophets into office. Not only are they in a position to pour out, but their circumstances give way for their ministry to flourish.

So realize that there is a lot more that the Holy Spirit is doing here than just dealing with your flesh. While you are on the cross, having all the dross brought up before your eyes, the Holy Spirit is fast at work ripping the veil in the temple and sending an earthquake to bring about the rearrangement.

Perhaps you have felt the shaking – perhaps you have not. For many, you come down from that cross wondering what exactly just happened. You went into your prayer closet one day and came out the next and the entire world had changed.

You wonder to yourself what God is up to. After all the training you have been through, you are ready for anything, but what is about to happen is different to what you have faced.

In this transition phase between training and prophetic office, the Lord is going to prepare the way for you! Just like Moses' mother made a basket and painted it with pitch, so also will the Lord begin to make preparations.

Isn't it something that when little Moses was put on the water to float, he was discovered by none other than the daughter of Pharaoh? Now that is God!

When the time is right for your release, the Lord will prepare the circumstances and you need to be aware of this change, or you could miss it.

I have seen some prophets be placed in office and within days, their circumstances began to change. Many misunderstood it. It was quite dramatic for some. I have seen the Lord move some prophets out of town… even to a different country right after being placed!

I have seen Him change their church or have them attend a new church. I have seen the Lord arrange circumstances in such a way that they end up joining an apostolic ministry and get direction from an apostle.

Now all of that takes time and planning. There is a lot more to get into line here than just your prophetic office. Other people are involved, and in addition to that, you need to be aware of it as well!

Because of the training phase you just went through, you can sometimes misunderstand this sudden change of circumstances! The disciples were expecting Jesus to take a Roman throne, not a heavenly one! It is the same with you. You have imagined what it would be like to be in office, but God has a very clear plan.

In the chapters to follow, I am going to talk about your place in the local and universal church, and how this will change when you reach office.

For now though, wait and watch! Be ready for what God has in mind and when the change in circumstances come, realize that it is the hand of God directing you.

KEY #3: POSITIONING OF RELATIONSHIPS

I mentioned this briefly already. Along with your circumstances, there is a lot that needs to change for your relationships to come in line with your calling as well. For most prophets, when they begin their journey, the Lord removes any relationships from them that will be a distraction.

Jesus left His hometown, and Paul left his family behind as well.

Any relationship that takes His place will be the first to be called to the altar. So you should be quite familiar with that part by now.

However, there have been a few relationships that have stuck with you through this process. Some have flourished and others have struggled. Before you reach office, realize that your calling affects those closest to you.

Your spouse, kids, and mentor are some of the people that also need to be prepared as you head to office. I have had some prophets halted in their training just before office, so that their spouse has some time to catch up! So if the Lord suddenly halts your training to work on relationships... take this very seriously!

If you are single, the Lord might even delay your training for a while, as He arranges circumstances for your future spouse. You must remember that the calling on your life will be added to by the calling on your spouse's life! What is the purpose of God giving you authority that you can never use, because your spouse opposes you?

Take time to get your relationships in order. As you submit to this direction from the Lord, you will see circumstances change. You will see your marriage come into line. There is no greater feeling than seeing your family follow you in the call.

I have given you a nicely rounded picture of what to expect in this transition from training to office, but before I get into understanding the fullness of prophetic authority, we are going to take a short detour in this book and flesh out this final "Key #3 Positioning of Relationships", because it is more vital than you realize!

CHAPTER 04

DEFINING THE PROPHETIC CHILD

Chapter 04 – Defining the Prophetic Child

Take my hand as I take you on a detour that will add a few missing pieces to the puzzle of this journey you have just been on. I understand that you are looking at reaching office and you might wonder what chapters on family and marriage are doing in this final book!

It is more essential than you realize. Consider this – where did your calling begin? Was it not the time that the Lord reached out to that little prophetic child that "fitted out" more than they "fitted in?"

So, we have now come a full circle. You are at the end of your race and the best way to cross that finish line is to remember where you started.

> **Key Principle**
>
> Now as the Lord called you to be a prophet, it is quite likely that your child also shares that calling.

Consider this chapter a two-fold blessing. Firstly, it will give you insight into what is going on with your child. Secondly, it is going to take you through a walk along memory lane, to help you conclude this race.

THE PROPHETIC CHILD DEFINED

> *Luke 1:76 "And you, child, will be called the prophet of the Highest; for you will go before the face of the Lord to prepare His ways,*
> *77 To give knowledge of salvation to His people by the remission of their sins,*
> *78 Through the tender mercy of our God, with which the Dayspring from on high has visited us;*
> *79 To give light to those who sit in darkness and the shadow of death, to guide our feet into the way of peace."*
> *80 So the child grew and became strong in spirit, and was in the deserts till the day of his manifestation to Israel.*

A PLANNED PREPARATION

If you have been through prophetic preparation, you've likely become more and more aware that you weren't just crazy your whole life. You didn't have a bad personality. In fact, it was a preparation that the Lord had put you through.

The isolation, the rejection, the pain you went through as a child, was pretty normal for a prophet of God. You saw that you weren't such an outcast after all. We have looked at the various stages of childhood, adolescence, and adulthood and of how you have grown up and were prepared to be a prophet of God (*Prophetic Boot Camp*).

Now, you were called from the womb. You were called out of the darkness of this world. What I am going to cover in this chapter is to look at the preparation of the child of a prophet.

There is a major difference between you and your child's preparation. This difference is that you, as a parent, play a very important role in creating and bringing your child up to be that prophet that he is called to be.

The first point is, how does the prophetic child come about? How do you identify whether your child is prophetic or not? What steps of preparation is your child going to follow? And finally, how do you go about aiding the call on your child's life, bringing him into maturity?

FAMILY GENERATIONAL BLESSING

Firstly, I'd like to go to the passage in 2 Timothy 1:5 where Paul says this to Timothy:

> *When I call to remembrance the genuine faith that is in you, which dwelt first in your grandmother Lois and your mother Eunice, and I am persuaded is in you also.*

It is passed down from generation to generation. The Lord has blessed you with this calling. He has brought you up in this calling, and He has given you an intensive time of preparation for it.

Just as curses are passed down from generation to generation, so blessings are passed down from generation to generation up to a thousand generations, the Scriptures say.

Defining the Prophetic Child

> **KEY PRINCIPLE**
>
> The blessing that is upon your life is a blessing that is going to be upon your child's life.

The calling that is on your life, very possibly, is going to be the calling on your child's life.

Now I know this, not just from the Word. I know this from personal experience. My grandparents and my father were prophets of God. They've moved mightily in prophetic ministry. Here I stand yet again, the third generation in those same shoes, as living proof that the blessing, ministry, and calling that is upon your life will overflow your heart and pour onto your children.

ON THE OUTSIDE LOOKING IN

So do not be astounded when your child suddenly starts acting weird on you. It's going to happen. You were weird, and people probably looked at you and said, "He's gone a little strange. He doesn't fit in with the rest of us."

Don't expect your child to be any different. When you start seeing him not fitting in with the rest of the crowd, you are likely to think, "Lord, what am I going to do with this child? He's socially inept."

Don't be discouraged. This is a good sign. What is happening, is what has been on you is pouring off onto your children, and you should identify it. It's something that you should rejoice in, and it's something that you should encourage.

Preparation of the Prophetic Child

I'd like to look at what steps of preparation the child goes through. You will identify with a lot of these, having gone through it yourself. I'd like to look at the scripture about John the Baptist that I quoted at the beginning.

1. Hidden Away

The very first point that you will see is that the prophetic child is hidden away. It says of John the Baptist that he was put into the desert until the time he was manifested to Israel. Your prophetic child will be hidden away. Do not expect your child to be popular. Do not expect him to fit in with the status quo. You didn't. How can you expect your child to do it?

You don't fit in with the status quo. You were kicked out of churches. People thought you were crazy. You never fitted in anywhere and were always the outcast.

Defining the Prophetic Child

> **KEY PRINCIPLE**
>
> Don't expect your child to fit in. Don't expect him to be something you never were, because it's part and parcel of his calling.

You know, I see this so often in parents, and I think we're all guilty of it to some extent. We expect things of our children that we cannot do ourselves. You expect your child to fit in with the church children. You expect your child to fit in with the kids at school.

You expect him to be elected for leadership positions, get A's in school, be a hotshot, and rise up in society so everybody can say, "Will you look at this! You've got such a magnificent son. Wow, you really brought him up well. Well done. You must be so proud."

It is not going to happen. The prophetic child is hidden away. He's hidden in the background. He's the little guy sitting in the back of the class that nobody notices. He's the little guy with no friends. Do you remember yourself as a child? That is your child. Don't expect anything more of him, because it is the way of the prophetic child.

You may say to me, "Why? It's not fair Lord. I hated it. It hurt. It was horrible and lonely. I cried myself to sleep at night. I sat in the playground all alone eating my lunch by myself and it was horrible. I felt like a nobody."

Your child is hidden away so that he may be hidden away from the enemy. You must realize that when your child grows up to maturity, he is going to be dynamic in the Kingdom of God. You need to realize that before he can be exposed to that, he needs to be hidden away to grow. If the devil has a foothold in his life at such a young age, he would destroy him.

What happened to Jesus when He was born? Mary and Joseph had to run and hide Him because Herod wanted to kill Him. Satan was out to destroy Him. Your child is going to do an amazing job in the Kingdom of God. Your child is going to be a weapon against the enemy.

Don't think the enemy will not want to take him out. So do not be discouraged if your child is hidden away. Do not be discouraged if he is hidden in the back seat of the class. Keep it in your heart, as Mary did. As you read through the Scriptures you see that she pondered those things in her heart. As a parent, ponder these things in your heart and know that your child is going to be so much bigger than you can perceive.

Don't try and push your child into a mold that he is not meant to be pushed into. Don't try to fit your child into a mold of your own hurts, experiences, and rejections, because you're just going to end up stopping the hand of the Lord in their lives, and you're going to be making it more difficult for the Lord to move them into their ministry faster.

2. Rejection

Your child is going to be rejected and cast down. Now, I know as a parent this must be one of the most difficult things to accept for our children. It's bad enough for them being isolated, but I know that when somebody says something nasty to my little girl, and she comes crying to me, I don't like it very much. I am a mom. It bothers me and it hurts. Your child is going to be rejected and cast down.

You just need to look at any of the prophets of old. Look at Joseph. He was rejected and cast down.

He said, "Man guys, look what the Lord showed me. I got this incredible vision. You won't believe it!"

He was so excited, but what happened?

They said, "Who do you think you are, you pathetic little squirt? You're the youngest of the lot of us. Get out of our way. What are you doing?"

His very own family rejected him. His very own father said to him, "Now come on, sort yourself out boy! You don't know what you're talking about. Will your mother and I bow down to you?"

You say, "But Lord, why the rejection? It's not fair. I went through it. It hurts. Why?"

Because if they're not rejected they will not have to look to Jesus to fill that space in their lives. If there isn't a need, it won't be filled. The Scripture says, "Ask and it shall be given to you, seek and you shall find, knock and the door shall be opened to you."

If the child doesn't look, he will not find. The Lord has to put the child in a place where he will look around and say, "How do I get this need filled? I'm rejected, I'm lost, I'm alone. How do I get it filled?" And he will look to the Lord.

That just opens the door wide for the Lord to reach down and say, "Here I am. I'm the one that's going to fill your need. I am the One that's going to lift you up. I am the answer to your cry."

Do not be discouraged when your child is rejected, when he is cast down, or when at school somebody else gets the promotion that he should have had.

I know it bothers you when other children are exalted in his place, when other children are nasty to him and don't want to play with him anymore, and when his very brothers and sisters turn against him and want nothing to do with him.

Don't be discouraged, because in that state of rejection and loneliness, he will go to his corner. It is in that corner that he will find Jesus. He will find the lover of his soul and his very best friend. It is in that little corner that he is going to find the answer to his need.

3. Sacrifice and Loss

Your child is going to be faced with situations of loss and sacrifice. The calling of a prophet is a very arduous one, and the Lord is very adamant about His prophets. He says, "Touch not mine anointed, and do my prophets no harm." He's very jealous over His people.

Anything that would come in the way of your child's calling, the Lord will remove. There is no cost too great that the Lord will not go to, to make sure that the child follows through in his calling to extend the Kingdom of God. The Kingdom of God comes first.

Look at Samuel. He was dropped off at the temple just after he was weaned. He was a little boy. All he knew was his mom, and he was dropped off at the temple with this old guy and... what now? Here he was in this strange place he had never been in before. His mother, who had been his sole supporter up until now, just left and came back only once a year to see him. He lost his family for the sake of the call. But it was there that he grew up to be one of the greatest prophets that ever lived. Loss and sacrifice were part of it.

If you look at Joseph, you think you had it bad? His brothers sold him as a slave. Talk about sacrifice! He lost his mom, his dad and his brothers. He even lost his freedom. You think your kid has it bad because the other kids pick on him at school? Hey, I got pretty bugged with my brother sometimes too, but I don't think I would ever ship him off to some slave traders.

> **KEY PRINCIPLE**
>
> Your child is going to suffer loss and sacrifice, but you must realize that it is for the extension of the Kingdom.

You must realize that everything that comes in the way of the calling, the Lord will remove. It's up to you, as a parent, to set his path straight. Put him on the right path to make sure that what the Lord wants, happens… to make sure that he is going in the right direction, to see what's happening, and to identify it.

I cannot stress this enough. It is so important that you identify this in your child's life and that you dare to encourage him and say, "You're not weird. It's okay. This is what's happening to you. This is what you are going through. It's exciting. It's a good thing. It means the Lord has something special in store for you!"

4. Pressure and Temptation

The final stage of the preparation of the prophetic child is more difficult for the parents than it is for the child. The final stage of the preparation before he comes into adulthood is where he faces pressure situations and temptations.

I get many letters and I hear lots of parents who say, "I don't know what I did wrong. I brought my child up in the Word, I've taken her to church, I've given everything I had and now, she's fourteen years old and she wants to run off and go to movies with her friends. She wants to go dancing at clubs. She's started drinking. You should hear the music she's listening to! Where did I go wrong? Lord, what did I do?"

You tear yourself up about it and say, "Is she ever going to come right? Have I wasted all my time? Is she lost to the world?"

You go into intercession, and put your request on all the prayer boards. You make an alert, "Pray for my daughter. She's gone wayward. Satan's got a grip on her."

You just need to realize that she's in the final stage of preparation. The Scriptures say that, "The Word of God is tried in the fire as gold." You need to realize that the Word has been put in her as you've brought her up. Those things that you've been putting in her year after year have to be burned in her heart - every sermon that you preached at her and she ignored. All the principles that you've said, "Now, how many times have I told you this…?" and she said, "Oh yeah, there's dad spouting off again."

It's not a simple case of just saying, "Yes, well my dad said that this is right. My dad said that this is the way it should be, and this is what my dad says." The conviction has to become her own.

CHAPTER 05

RAISING A PROPHETIC CHILD

Chapter 05 – Raising a Prophetic Child

The hardest part of raising a prophetic child? Feeling like the worst failure as a parent in the world. With each rejection, you trigger back to your own childhood and wish you could save them from it.

It is around this point that you start to bring an imbalance and instead of helping them move forward in the call you become their greatest hindrance. I have seen prophets in office make the biggest mistakes with their kids for a number of reasons.

The first being – they do not want their child to have the experiences they had.

The second is, that they see in their child the same "quirky" characteristics that they have and handle that incorrectly. Either they excuse the flesh, or they try to shape the child into something God never intended.

So the first thing you need to do when raising a prophetic child is… calm down! You made it through, didn't you? The Lord never left you in the dark, all alone and neither will He leave your child in the dark.

He is their God and Savior… not you!

> **KEY PRINCIPLE**
>
> You cannot be your child's "Holy Spirit." You can only be their mother or father.

There are many things that you cannot save your child from, but what you can do is be the person that they can lean on when they face the storms.

You can protect them from the attacks of the enemy and you can arm them for the battles they will face. So having raised a few of these children myself, I hope to give you some practical tips. For those that have "been there" you will relate to what I am going to share.

1. GET OVER YOURSELF

This is not about you – this is about their calling. This is not about you failing or succeeding as a parent. This is about a mighty warrior that was chosen from the womb. From the moment you felt their first kick, the Lord had His hand on their lives and there is nothing you can do to take that away.

You can be the worst mother or father in the world, and it will not matter. God will still call your child and woo them unto Himself. If God could take you out of such difficult circumstances and you were all alone, how much more can He do for your child?

It is not the world or even the enemy that is your child's greatest hindrance. Their greatest hindrance is you! Your hopes, dreams, and ambitions for your child. Each of those ambitions is based on what you do not want them to have.

How can you shape the life of a child with what you do not want them to have? When the Lord created Adam, He formed Him in His image. He did not say, "Let us create Him in what is not our image!"

You cannot raise your child on one hand, while trying to raise them to *not* have something you had! You can only invest the good into them, based on the image that God has given to them.

If you raise your child in fear, you will conform them to that fear. Raise them instead according to the picture that God has given to you for them. Then you have something positive to start with.

When Mary brought Jesus to the temple she was told that a sword would pierce her heart. It was a hint towards the pain that she would feel as she saw her eldest son bleeding on the cross. One can imagine the heartbreak of a mother, watching the one she loved bleeding and broken.

She felt his first kick. She remembered him falling asleep at her breast and there she stood watching Him bleed out in front of her. Do you think that she found it any easier than you do today, seeing the road your child will walk?

Yet she never stood in His way – even though she knew what would happen. He had a destiny that she had a part to play in, but she could not walk the way out for Him. Neither can you walk out your child's call, but you can certainly prepare them for that journey so that they can walk it without falling.

2. Identify Their Abilities and Limitations

Once you can get over yourself and what you want your child to become, seeing what the Lord has put into them is quite easy. Until you see both their strengths and limitations, you have no starting place.

Abilities

Their abilities will become clear from a young age. Deborah-Anne (my eldest) just had a sensitivity to the spirit that I could not explain. I never had to sit her down one day and say "Jesus is with you" because she was always aware of His presence. All I had to do was give a name to what she already felt.

When I taught her about Jesus, she recognized the peace she felt and the Lord she was already conversing with. It was not uncommon for her to sneak off during the day to have some "alone time" with Jesus. She was drawn to Him. She had a connection to the Spirit that I did not understand at first.

She was the kind of child that did not wait for me to teach her how to read... she asked the Lord Jesus and He taught her. She just "saw" people. She did not find it difficult to identify with how they felt or to reach out to them.

When it came to prayer or times in the spirit, she could get lost in it. The Lord was already trying to woo her and seeing these strengths was simple. Of course, there were some hiccups along the way.

There was the time I was trying my utmost to teach her math and she kept "going off" into the spirit. Then suddenly it occurred to me what was happening and I had to snap her back to reality and say, "Deborah! You are not going to get the answer by revelation. You actually have to think and use your brain for this!"

She was just so dependent on the Lord that she thought every answer was found in the Spirit. She was in "another world" all the time. Often I had to snap her back to reality. She would get so lost in her make-believe world that she did not hear or see anyone around her. Yeah… she may have taken on some of her mother's prophetic weaknesses!

That "black and white" thinking did not endear her to many others and before long, rejection followed her like a fragrance – as it does for all of us called to the prophetic.

The thing is, I could not impose strengths on her that I wanted her to have! I had to recognize the strengths God had given to her. God gave her an ability to talk to people and He gave her eyes to see. He did not gift her with tact. He did not gift her with a scientific mind!

I could not try to make her into what I wanted. I had to recognize what was her ability and what was not. Only then, could I teach her to stand on that. Ok, so she was not a great mathematical genius, but from a young age, she could write and even started writing her own book at 15. God could use that and so He has as the years have passed.

Identify your child's real strengths and not the ones you wish that they had. From there, you have a starting point.

Limitations/Flaws

A word of caution – no parent likes to admit that their child has any failures. Then if they are willing to admit it, they get upset if anyone else points those flaws out. Crazy isn't it?

The thing is, until you see their limitations, how can you arm them for the future? Why are you getting so upset at people pointing out the weaknesses in your child that you see for yourself?

The answer to that question – you feel guilty. Yup... it is all about you again, isn't it? You are upset that others tease your child or expose their flaws, because it makes you feel like a failure as a parent. You get so hung up on that, that you cannot help your child to overcome.

So let's start with a new slate. Let's start with looking at what needs work. So yes, let me use my daughter again. She is gracious and with a heart for prophetic children everywhere, she will not be too mad at me for penning her to paper once more!

While Deborah loved the Lord and her little world of safety, she did not respond to rejection well. Some people fight back when rejected – but she was not one of those. After a while, she started to withdraw into herself.

She also had a quick mouth (Gee, I wonder who she got that from?) She would always open it and say something she shouldn't. Tact was never her friend. She also had a hard time taking correction and every time she was corrected - she would give a hundred excuses as to why she messed up.

The reason of course, is that she did not handle rejection well and saw every correction as a rejection! Yes, she was not different to many prophetic children today, going through the throes of preparation.

Each one handles it differently. Some of the rejection comes because of their call. Some of the rejection comes just because of their character flaws that ask for it! Now what are you going to do? Are you going to say, "My poor child! They cannot help that they shoot their mouth off and say things they should not?" or are you going to teach your child to use tact?

Here are some of the ways that a prophetic child will respond to the pressures of rejection and prophetic preparation:

- Rebellion against authority
- Escape into the things of the world
- Bitterness and anger
- Over-emotion to try and get attention
- Pushiness to take control and tell others what to do
- Fear to step out – they will run away from the world and everyone else
- Tantrums to get attention
- Pushing people away deliberately to avoid hurt

The list goes on, but I am sure that you already see a few of these characteristics in your child. Now look, I know that a prophetic child faces preparation because of their calling, but we really can reduce collateral damage here!

There is something we can do as parents to help them face the winds and the waves. We can also teach them to avoid the storms by helping them work on their character flaws, now.

So with that being said, let's see what you can do right now to help your child through this transition.

3. Lay a Foundation

Now I do not want to go into a whole lesson on raising children. Rather I want to make it specific for the prophetic child - a child that is geared for leadership in the church. It stands to reason then, that they need to learn the lessons that you did and those lessons began with…submission, obedience and servanthood!

Your child is your first disciple, so it is up to you to lay a spiritual and doctrinal foundation in them that will give them the upper hand as they go through their training one day.

Imagine if you had begun with all of this already in place?

SUBMISSION

> ***1 Timothy 3:4** one who rules his own house well, having his children in submission with all reverence*

Submission to authority is essential and as we continue talking about prophetic ministry and marriage, you will learn more about this. Until your child can learn to submit to and respect the authority in this world, how will they respect and submit to the Lord?

Do not think that if you teach your child to rebel against the authorities in the world and in the home, that they will grow up suddenly respecting God. The Father is the first authority in the home and as a child is taught (by the mother) to respect that authority, the child will respect the Lord also.

> **KEY PRINCIPLE**
>
> Submission means simply to choose to follow someone else's will instead of your own.

Are you teaching your child submission? If you undermine the authorities set over you, I promise it is the same example you are teaching your child. It will mean that they will have to deal with that later in their training. You can save them from it now, by laying the right foundation from the beginning!

OBEDIENCE

> ***Ephesians 6:1*** *Children, obey your parents in the Lord, for this is right*

Not a very popular word in today's society is it? Mostly, we are told to raise our kids to be "happy," not obedient. Then suddenly they become adults and must obey the Word of God. However, if you did not teach them to be obedient in the many realms of leadership in the world, then how can you expect them to obey God?

Remember how much you had to be brought to the cross time and again regarding obedience? You can make it so much easier for your child by teaching them the power of obedience now. Obedience to his leaders and obedience to the Lord. As you walk in this obedience yourself, you will see the fruit in your child!

SERVANTHOOD

> ***Philippians 2:7*** *but made Himself of no reputation, taking the form of a bondservant, and coming in the likeness of men*

The ultimate power of leadership – servanthood! Have you asked your child what they have done today to serve others? Does he realize that servanthood is the highest form of worship to the Lord?

If your child is not taught this skill in the home, where do you expect him to learn it? Will the Lord need to bring along another spiritual parent to teach them? I work with quite a diverse team and I can really tell who had parents that taught them submission, obedience and servanthood – they were the easiest to work with.

Sure, they still had to be taken through the rigors of prophetic training. However, because they already had that solid foundation, they moved through their training at a record pace. You can do your child that favor as well!

Instead of excusing their bad attitude and negative responses to the rejection, you can give them a foundation that will serve them later in life. Do not overlook their limitations! Do not allow sin to take root.

On the other hand, do not wish that they were just "normal" because they will never be "normal" – they are your child after all!

4. Arm Them for Battle

Do you remember everything I taught you in *Prophetic Essentials* and *Prophetic Functions*? These are not principles just for an adult – they work for a child as well! Everything you learned about templates and triggers in *Prophetic Boot Camp* applies to your child as well!

The only difference is that you can watch them make those templates right before your eyes.

Nothing quite prepares you for the first time your child comes home with tears streaming down their cheeks because the kids in the neighborhood picked on them. Nothing prepares you for seeing others lash out at your child and seeing the hurt on their face.

The mother or father in you, wants to die for them. The greatest mistake you can make is to jump in and say, "It is not your fault. They are just horrible people."

It is what you really want to say… but that is not going to help. They need the Word and what does the Word say? It says that if we are slapped on one cheek we turn the other.

It says that we must rejoice in affliction. Remember how badly you responded to those rejections? Remember how long it took you to work through your sinful responses? Save them the struggle! Teach them to handle rejection properly. You will do that by telling them that they do not wrestle with flesh and blood!

You will tell them that, "It's true. Life is not fair, but you are never alone. You do not need to fear and you do not need to respond in bitterness. You can ask the Lord Jesus to help you love them back."

Then you can put your arms around them and comfort them. However, make sure that you have taught them first, how to respond, based on the Word.

Flowing in the Spirit

> **Key Principle**
>
> Your child's greatest defense against the enemy is their relationship with the Lord Jesus.

Ok, I am not going to sugarcoat it – I was a tough mom. When Deborah hit her teen years and the "hire a teenager while they know everything" started manifesting I did not mince my words.

She would come downstairs with attitude and before she made it across the room I would say, "Go right back upstairs and go sort your spirit out. Go talk to the Lord and come to peace. Once you have sorted that oppression, you can come back down and join us."

Tough? Perhaps… but she did it. She had grown up with a relationship with Jesus and she knew exactly who her Savior was. Until you bring your child into a face-to-face relationship with Jesus, they are facing a battle that will overcome them.

You cannot always be there to protect them! You cannot always be there to comfort them – but Jesus can. Just as you have learned to enter into a face-to-face relationship with the Lord. Pass that beautiful inheritance onto your child.

Teach them to come to peace. Teach them to hear the voice of the Lord for themselves. My son, only six, was very restless. There was obviously a lot going on and I asked him what was going on. He said, "It is like I am so hungry and so thirsty inside, but I am not really hungry or thirsty for real." He was feeling conflict in the spirit, but could not understand it.

I could explain what was going on so that he could come to peace. I told him to close his eyes and to see the Lord Jesus right there with him. Jesus was holding him and telling him how precious he was. It's really that simple. Children know the Lord instinctively. Just introduce them to Jesus and He will do the rest.

STANDING ON THE WORD

The more you feed good morals and political correctness into your child, the more they will have to work on when they hit training. Do them a favor and allow the Word to become their standard. When Deborah came home seething mad because of what someone said to her, it was not the time to tell her that she was right. Sure, the rejection was unjust. Sure, the other person was completely in the wrong.

That was not the point though, was it? The point was her response. The Word tells us to be angry, but not to sin. It tells us that we should respond to cursing with the force of love. Becoming bitter because of a rejection was not the correct solution.

By all means, keep your convictions, but respond to the rejection correctly! Don't you wish you could have done that? The Word should be the basis for your response.

It's simple actually. Every time you give your child an instruction, ask yourself this, "What scripture confirms the instruction I just gave that child?" Did I tell him, "Just ignore them, they do not know what they are talking about?" or did I tell him, "Just because you do not agree, does not give you the right to be bitter. Stand firm in your convictions, but do not respond with bitterness!"

The principles you are learning are as good for your child as they are for you. Walking in faith, hope, and love is not just something for adults – but for kids also. As the Lord has taken you through your training and now as you walk out your call, allow your child to become your disciple.

Allow them to identify their sinful responses throughout life. Teach them to respond correctly. Take them through inner healing. Above all else, introduce them to Jesus and teach them to hear His voice for themselves. If you fail at all else, cling to that one thing, for then you will find that the Holy Spirit will take over where you end off.

CHAPTER 06

PROPHETIC MARRIAGE: HUSBANDS

Chapter 06 – Prophetic Marriage: Husbands

> **Romans 16:3** *Greet Priscilla and Aquila, my fellow workers in Christ Jesus,*
> *4 who risked their own necks for my life, to whom not only I give thanks, but also all the churches of the Gentiles.*
> *5 Likewise greet the church that is in their house.*

When my relationship with my husband and my relationship with the Lord are secure, then I can do anything that God wants me to do.

There is no demon of darkness that can come against me when I have got my husband and the Lord standing behind me. That is why I love the picture I see in the New Testament of Priscilla and Aquila. Our first marriage team!

It was no secret that Peter also travelled and ministered with his wife, but what we have here is a couple that is mentioned side by side.

They are our first proof of the first real ministry team in the New Testament!

A Good Marriage Makes - A Bad Marriage Breaks

So let me kick this chapter off with a challenge. How much time have you spent developing your relationship in your marriage? I tell you, a good marriage can make your ministry, but a bad marriage can break it.

If you are suffering in your marriage right now and if you know it is not where you need it to be, then stop and work on it.

All that satan needs to do is to just bring up one of those little issues in the middle of ministry to destroy your ministry completely. I even consider the experience of my own parents.

My mother loved the Lord. She was born again from a very young age, spirit-filled at the age of four. This is not somebody who didn't love the Lord. She loved the Lord. I come from quite a few generations of Christians. They all loved the Lord. That's what we did, we loved the Lord. We did the work of the ministry.

There came a time though where she got to a point where she did not want to move forward any longer. My father, being married to the ministry first and his wife second, did not see the early warning signs. How could anything be wrong?

God comes first, then the ministry, then your wife… right?

God comes first, then your ministry, then your husband… right?

There is something seriously amiss with that equation and like so many other leadership couples in today's church society – my mother broke. She did not want to be third in line. She could not live up to the expectation.

She made some huge mistakes and broke their marriage covenant in the hopes of finding the attention she craved so much in the arms of someone else.

Our world fell apart and through the storms of that season, the reality of how marriage is core to every ministry foundation, came to the forefront.

You cannot force someone to take on the call of God. However, if you are going to move forward, you are not making headway without your spouse being in agreement.

Yes, the Lord should always be first, but realize that marriage is a covenant vow.

> **KEY PRINCIPLE**
> Your first covenant is with the Lord. The second is with your spouse. Reality check: ministry is not a covenant act.

Your ministry is a vehicle. Preaching behind the pulpit on Sunday is a vehicle. It is just one way that you can minister and fulfill your purpose and it should not come before your spouse.

How many leaders have we seen who put their ministry above marriage and family? So then the family of Christ comes ahead of your own family? Hmm…. Let's review this passage then:

> **1 Timothy 3:5** *for if a man does not know how to rule his own house, how will he take care of the church of God?*

Before you qualify to stand up and take care of the house of God, your house must be cared for first.

Unfortunately, in a world where you face so much rejection, it is just too easy to have your needs met in ministry. Again… do you see why the Lord has taken you out of active ministry for a little while?

He needed to set you aside for a season so that your needs could rise up and you could get them met in the Lord. Now is also the time to work on your relationship with your spouse!

LET'S GET REAL

So, you already know that if you are going to make it to prophetic office that your family and marriage situation has to come into line first. So what can you do right now to speed up this process?

Well, I am going to look at both sides, and I am sharing this with the worst case scenario because it happens. Let's just be real here, okay?

The first thing I am going to teach you is how to bring reconciliation to divisions in your marriage. However, I also want you to know that if you have gone through a divorce, if you have failed, then not only is God willing to forgive you, but he wants you to have the opportunity to start over again with the right foundation.

I want to give you this picture of what it should look like. If you are looking to the Lord right now for a husband or a wife whether you are single, have been divorced, or widowed, you need to know these principles.

I want to help you avoid the pitfalls in your marriage right now. As the Lord starts bringing all the pieces together for you, do not rush through this final relationship phase of your training. Take your time to invest into your marriage and family.

Before you know it, resurrection of your vision will take place. The doors will open and silence will make way for too many demands on your time. Do not rush this season! Take the time now to make it right, before you fall headlong into the same mistakes so many before you have made.

THE PROPHETIC MARRIAGE – A TUG-OF-WAR

You want to go into ministry. He is dragging his heels. You are on fire for God and wanting to become a prophet – she refuses to acknowledge your call or support you.

Here you are wanting to serve the Lord and it feels to you that your spouse is not as spiritual as you, and keeps dragging their feet. You have got all these ambitions, you want to rise up, and they are just so phlegmatic about the whole thing.

Let me break it down to two very simple points.

There are two rules to marriage - two commandments given.

> ***Ephesians 5:25*** *Husbands, love your wives, just as Christ also loved the church and gave Himself for her*

> ***Ephesians 5:22*** *Wives, submit to your own husbands, as to the Lord*

HUSBANDS, LOVE YOUR WIVES

How did Christ love the Church? He loved her enough to die for her. He loved her enough that even when they rejected Him, that even when they put nails in Him, that even when they accused Him and put a spear in His side... He still said, "Father, forgive them."

Not only that, He rose from the dead so that through His name they might be saved. Those same ones that stuck the thorns in Him and nailed Him to the cross, were given the same liberty to walk in the new covenant as His disciples that never gave up hope.

That is the love of Christ and that is the love husbands are required to love their wives with.

It Does NOT have to be fair!

"But you don't know my wife, she is vindictive. She is so dominating - she does not even give me a chance to say what I think. She does not consider what I feel at all."

Yes. So were the Roman soldiers that nailed Jesus to the cross. Do you think that was fair? Do you think that was fair that He had to die for sins that He never committed?

Do you think it was fair that He had to be beaten the way He was? Do you think it was fair the way they made fun of Him and laughed in His face, and spat at Him?

I never told you it had to be fair. I said, "This is the Word of God."

Key Principle

> The Word of God says, "Husbands, love your wives" regardless of what she says, or does.

Come now! I am not talking to a new covert here. I am talking to a prophet who is rather familiar with the concept of seeing things in "black and white."

This is pretty straight forward. Do you love your wife above all else, or is she there for your convenience? Is your love for her greater than your love for your ministry?

THE CORRECT ORDER

> ***Ephesians 5:28*** *So husbands ought to love their own wives as their own bodies; he who loves his wife loves himself*

You see, it is like this:

1. You love the Lord, your God with all of your heart.
2. Secondly, you love your wife as you do your own body
3. In third place - you love your ministry.

Do you see that order? Lord, wife, and ministry at the very end. "But I am doing the work of God so therefore that takes preeminence." No, you are not doing the work of God, you are meeting your own need. You are chasing after what you want to do and makes you feel good about yourself.

Do me a favor and let the Lord take care of His ministry.

When you love like that, God covers your back. I have seen Him transform marriages. You do your part and God will do His.

Love is a very powerful force. When you love that way, it releases the will of God into that person. The Lord will not override their will, but He will try to woo them.

He will try to change them. He will reach out to them and then it is up to that person to decide which way they are going to go.

Your Wife: Your First Ministry

Your responsibility, if you really want to bring change to your wife, is to forget about your ministry and start ministering to her. Let her be your number one ministry. Learn to love her and meet her need for acceptance. When last were you more of a pastor in the home than you were behind the pulpit?

When was the last time you brought your wife flowers? When was the last time you took her out for dinner? When was the last time you surprised her with something she wasn't expecting?

When was the last time you dropped everything just to say, "Let's go for a walk? What is going on in your life right now?"

When was the last time you loved as Christ loved and said, "I understand" even when she said or did things that hurt and were not fair? I am not saying that you need to be a pushover. I am not saying that you need to let go of your commitment in the Lord or your God-given authority in the home. That's not what love is.

Love is a very powerful force. Love does not rejoice in any evil, it believes all things, it hopes all things, and it covers sin.

Remember back to your courting days. When was the last time you did candlelight and roses? Is this teenage stuff? Is that only the stuff that you did when you were courting?

Women Love Words

Let me let you in on a secret, guys. Women are emotional creatures. "Well, I bought her a set of pots for her birthday. She should appreciate that."

She doesn't.

She is not feeling your love through the pots and pans. She's not a man. A woman feels love through words. She craves to be noticed.

That's why the Lord wrote so much in the Scriptures. He knew how much we needed words. The problem is that when you are working so hard in your ministry, your wife is going to feel neglected.

Now if she is feeling neglected because of all the fuss you are making over your ministry (instead of her), how much do you think she is going to want to be a part of what you are doing? Will she love you and your ministry more? No, it is going to put her back up and she is not going to want to have anything to do with your ministry.

How Does Your Wife Feel Around You?

So, let's swing the balance. Perhaps, she isn't as spiritual as you. Love her anyway. Give her a reason to want to be with you.

I'll leave you with this one question: How does your wife feel when she is around you?

When your wife is around you she shouldn't be sitting listening to how great you are doing. She should feel good about herself when she is around you. She should be feeling on top of the world.

If she felt that good about herself, if she felt that good every time she was around you, she is going to want to be around you more often. She is going to want to hear what you have to say more often. She is going to want to be a part of what you are doing more often, because every time she is around you, she just feels so good.

Come on. This is reality here. Through all the preparation and training that we go through, we sometimes lose sight of the things that are most important to us.

You Need Good Relationships

We get so busy on the ministry track that we forget the importance of those that are close to us. Let me tell you, without these relationships in your life to bring joy - your ministry is lacking.

> **Key Principle**
>
> Without the joy that comes from a good marriage relationship, your ministry is missing a huge piece.

It is one thing to have the anointing. You can stand up there and be anointed, but what happens when you come down from the pulpit? What happens when the anointing leaves? Who are you then? What do you have then?

The greatest treasure that we have is in the relationships God has given to us.

Let's smash the "either/or" thinking. It is not, "I have my ministry or I have my marriage." It is, "I have my ministry *and* my marriage."

They are one and the same. Marriage is like a triangle. You are on the one side, your spouse on the other, and God is on the top. The closer you get to God, the closer you get to each other. When you get to the top, you have a threefold cord that cannot be broken.

Husbands, love your wives. Really. Regardless of what she says, does, is, likes, or does not like. Take your eyes off yourself for a while and put them onto her. You are so busy putting your eyes onto ministering to others. You are so busy meeting everybody else's needs. You are so busy being there for the Lord, being there for the congregation, being there for people.

How about being there for the one person in this world that needs you the most? Are you prepared to die for her? Are you prepared to live for her?

CHAPTER 07

PROPHETIC MARRIAGE: WIVES

Chapter 07 – Prophetic Marriage: Wives

Remember the two rules? Husbands, love your wives. Wives, submit to your husband. Looking at society today, you would imagine that it is the other way around. You keep loving your husband, wondering why he will not submit!

You end up in a tug of war, because he will not let go of what he wants, to do what you want. I ask you… when will he just learn to submit? The catch being of course, that God put the man as the head of the home and not the other way around.

Now I am not talking here about strength, talent, or ability. I am talking about an order. Being strong and being submissive are not the same thing. You can be strong and you can still submit.

The Submission Definition

Because just like I said to the men that love is the power, let me tell you ladies, "Submission is power. Submission is the greatest power you can ever have over your man."

Doesn't that sound crazy? It is in a man's heart to want to be loved, respected, admired, to be looked up to, and to be trusted. You see that is what submission is, isn't it?

It is not just agreeing with him. Anybody can agree. Your boss tells you, "I want you to come into the office an hour earlier tomorrow." You can submit to that instruction. You may not like it, but you make the choice to follow the instruction.

Submission is Not Simply "Agreement"

Submission is not about being devoid of an opinion. Let's look at Ephesians 5:22 again. Take a look at the Greek for the word "submit" there.

> 5293 hupotasso {hoop-ot-as'-so}
>
> AV - put under 6, be subject unto 6, be subject to 5, submit (one's) self unto 5, submit (one's) self to 3, be in subjection unto 2, put in subjection under
>
> 1) to arrange under, to subordinate
>
> 2) to subject, put in subjection
>
> 3) to subject one's self, obey
>
> 4) to submit to one's control
>
> 5) to yield to one's admonition or advice
>
> 6) to obey, be subject
>
> A Greek military term meaning "to arrange [troop divisions] in a military fashion under the command of a leader." In non-military use, it was "a voluntary attitude of giving in, cooperating, assuming responsibility, and carrying a burden."

The part about this definition I love the most is that this is, in fact, a military term. In every single definition, I want you to notice something. Submission is a choice. It means to deliberately put yourself under someone else's authority.

Do you see anything there about "feelings" or "character"? Does it say anything about being a mindless drone without ideas and feelings of your own?

No, submission is the ultimate act of love because it says, "I have an idea of what I want to do. You have an idea of what you want to do. Because I love you... we are going to do it your way!"

SUBMISSION OF WILLS

Suddenly why submission is so powerful, comes to light. The Lord tells us to submit to our husbands as unto the Lord. How many times has the Lord asked something of you that you really did not want to do?

I do not know about you, but I have been there many times myself! There were times when the Lord asked me to do something that I really did not want to do! It cut against my flesh and my will. It was uncomfortable.

However, at the end of the day, I love Him so much that I choose His way instead of my own. Sure... it does not mean I loved it, but it does mean that I submitted to Him because I loved Him.

This is what the Lord is asking of you today. Not to submit because "it is the right thing to do." Rather, it means choosing your husband's will over your own, because of love.

Is there any greater show of love than that of Jesus in the Garden of Gethsemane? Sweating blood, He sought His Father saying, "Lord if only this cup could pass from me..." Do you think Jesus wanted to die such a brutal death? He was a man like you and me. He was afraid of it! He travailed in that garden! Yet in the end, what does He say? "Father, not my will... but yours be done."

If Jesus could submit to the Father unto death, surely you and I can submit to our husbands unto the death of getting things our way?

We value the relationships where the other person loves you so much to let you have your way. This is the kind of love that He calls you to love your husband with. When you love this way, you grant honor, respect, and trust.

You are saying, "I am not a mindless fool. I have opinions. I am very strong and capable. However, I have decided that your idea is the better one and I am choosing to think that you are better than me. I am trusting that you see something that I do not."

GRANTING HONOR

Honor falls very much into the same category as submission. It means choosing to look at what deserves honor instead of what does not.

How does your husband feel when he is around you? Does he feel like the most important man in the world? Does he feel like he is so strong and capable?

When you speak about your husband to other people, are you bragging about him or are you tearing him down?

I am not trying to put a guilt trip on you. I want you to tap into the greatest power you have. Perhaps your husband doesn't seem so super-spiritual. He is not spiritual enough for you. But you know, he is a human being and he is your husband and he loves you. He might not have your strengths, but there are other skills that God has given him.

Recognizing Your Differences

I have seen so many women in the prophetic who are so desperate for their husbands to *be* something, that they call them apostles. "Wow, God has called my husband to be an apostle. He just hasn't stepped into the calling yet." No, God has not called your husband to be an apostle.

You think that by saying, "God has called my husband to be an apostle" it somehow justifies your prophetic ministry. Leave your poor husband alone! You are pushing him into a role God never intended and it is going to backfire because he cannot meet up to those expectations in your mind.

WELL-PLACED EXPECTATION

Let him be who he is. Just love him and accept him for who he is right now. Let it go! And I tell you, ladies, when you do that such a load is going to lift off your shoulders.

You keep expecting him to be something he never will be. Then you are devastated because your expectation was dashed. Well, what did you expect? You placed a false expectation on him.

By all means, expect of him what God tells you to, but be sure it is what God expects and not just what you want.

> **KEY PRINCIPLE**
>
> Letting go of false expectations is the greatest relief you will ever experience.

I had a frustrated wife come to me once with a list of everything her husband was not doing. He was just not participating in the ministry and her expectations were dashed again and again. So I said, "Well then, it is time to expect less of him isn't it?"

Now before you get all up in arms – think about it. You have all these high expectations in the wrong places, and then cannot understand why you are crushed! Have lower expectations in the areas where he is weak and higher expectations in the areas where he is strong. The balance will swing.

Good news though – that wife did follow my instruction and now the two of them stand side by side doing the work of God. Neither of them do the same thing. Turns out that her husband had strengths all of his own that did not match hers!

So perhaps your husband is not so super-spiritual. Reality check: He doesn't need to be. You make up enough spirituality for the both of you!

Maybe he needs to be a bit more naturalistic in his thinking. Maybe you need him to be a little bit more logical because you are not. You need him to be more down-to-earth because you are always up in the clouds.

Together… what a team. You need both sides of the coin.

"Oh, my husband is also a prophet, he is also an apostle, and he is this great big hero. He just doesn't know it yet because he won't hear God. He is just not spiritual enough for me."

Do you know what the worst part is? That is how your husband feels when he is around you all the time. He feels, "I am not spiritual enough for her. I am not what she wants me to be." He doesn't feel respected. He doesn't feel admired.

Let's be frank. If all you ever felt was guilty or unworthy around somebody all the time, would you want to be around them?

THAT VOTE OF CONFIDENCE

When was the last time that you gave your husband a vote of confidence? When was the last time you said, "I believe in you" and "wherever you go, I will follow"? You see, when you do that, you put a weight on your husband's shoulders.

He now doesn't just have to care for his own problems, but he has to care for yours as well.

I have a lot of people writing in, all frustrated, because their husband wants to go to a church, but they have just decided that they don't like the church and so they are going to a different one.

Couples going to different churches! Why serve the Lord at all? You are supposed to be one, and if you cannot even be one in the spirit, then forget about the rest.

If you can't even be in agreement with the most basic principle such as serving the Lord at a church, how will you ever start a ministry together? Ladies, I hate to break it to you, but the Word is clear: It is for wives to submit. If your husband wants to go to that horrible church that you don't like - you better trust God in him.

You know what? It could be worse! He could not be wanting to go to church at all. How many women are struggling out there with unsaved husbands who don't even want to serve the Lord? Here you are quibbling about which church he wants to go to?

Don't you think God can use you in that church? Don't you think that God has a bigger plan than what you can see? Is it all about your entertainment and about how you like praise and worship?

Maybe there is a work waiting right there for you in the middle of the church that you don't like.

"No, I have my rights. This is what God is telling me. Just forget my husband." You know what you have done? You have just erased him right out of your ministry. Then when you want to move forward, you don't understand why he doesn't want to support you.

Did you support him? Did you give him that vote of confidence?

We don't realize the power that we have as women. I know that I am being harsh on you and that I am on my little soapbox, but you know what? I can afford to be on my soapbox because I have walked this road. I am strong and I know the price God has called us to pay. I know that it can be paid and I know that there is power in paying it.

REAL CHANGE

You see, the Lord has placed your husband as the covering of the home. I don't care how many scriptures you try to go through - the Word is clear.

> **KEY PRINCIPLE**
>
> The husband is placed as the covering of the home. Deal with it, face it. The Word of God stands. It is your reality.

So the ladder looks like this: The Lord at the top with your husband directly under him. What happens if you are not right beneath your husband, but somewhere out in the middle of nowhere?

You are receiving from God all by yourself, with your husband standing on his own. Then you can't understand why you are not involved in his life?

Here is where the power is: The Lord is on top of the ladder, followed by your husband, then you standing neatly in line under that.

When you have a spiritual need, God will need to go through your husband to get to you. Guess what? The Lord will continue to work through your husband, for as long as you stay in place.

That is where real change will come. By you coming to the place of submission, right under your husband, he will have no choice but to change. Not because you said so, but because God needs to get to you. To get to you, He needs to go through him.

God's Part

Submission is power. Love is power. If we do things according to God's pattern and according to the Word, we can expect Him to back us up. We can expect Him to do what we cannot do.

Your marriage is more important than you realize. I don't want you to lose hope. I want you to be challenged by what I have shared. I hope I made you mad at least once. I hope I made you disagree with me at least once because if something hit you, then you can be sure that God is pulling something out there.

I want you to say, "Lord, your will be done on earth as it is in heaven. Not my will, not what I want, but your will be done."

To walk in real love, to walk in real submission, and to give God some authority in your marriage.

Something for the Singles

Before I end this chapter, I want to mention a few principles for all you singles out there. Whether you have never been married, or have gone through the pain of divorce, I want to let you know that the Lord has a spouse for you who will walk out this call!

The Two Guidelines

If you are looking for somebody to serve the Lord with, you need two guidelines. I know that you have made your list of everything you want in your spouse, but there are two points that you can boil them all down to:

1. Somebody that loves the Lord.
2. Somebody that adores you.

If you have these two things on your list of "the perfect spouse," the Lord can do anything with you as a couple. Decide that what is most important is to love the Lord with all your heart and all your mind, and to love one another just as passionately. Then the Lord can do anything with you.

MARRIAGE IS A GIFT AND PROMISE

I really believe that in this day and age the Lord is raising up ministry teams. Maybe you even asked, "Should I get married? Why should I get married?" Perhaps you faced a painful divorce. I want you to know that it was not His will for you to be broken. It was not his will for you to suffer loss. It is His will for you to have that need met!

God created the marriage relationship because He knew our hearts. Even Adam, who was the perfect man, could not be alone. Even Jesus Christ, who is the perfect son of God, needs a bride. If Jesus Christ, the perfect one, needs a bride, how much more, you and I.

God made us this way. It is natural. It is nothing to be afraid of. But, make sure that when you make that step, it is somebody that will do anything for the Lord. Is it somebody that says, "Lord, use me. Lord, I want to do anything you want me to"? Also, make sure that it somebody that loves you.

If that potential spouse has these two qualities, then you have found yourself a catch. You have not just found yourself a spouse, you found yourself a team member. You would have found yourself somebody that will do the work of God with you.

With this kind of commitment, it doesn't depend on you. When they do what God wants them to do, then God can speak to them.

If you are a single looking for somebody, I want you to remember those points and burn them on your heart because God wants the best for you. He wants somebody to not just be there for your needs, but He also wants somebody that He will use to melt the two of you together until you can't tell the one from the other.

It is possible! There is hope! Don't let go of that hope no matter where you are!

KNOW WHAT TO EXPECT

Have this picture clearly in your mind. As a wife, you are going to come into full submission to whomever you marry. Is the man you are going to marry someone who loves the Lord? If so, you don't ever have to fear trusting him. You won't have to fear because he loves the Lord and the Lord can take him anywhere.

If you are looking for a wife, is this somebody that loves the Lord? This is somebody who you are going to have to love and pour out to. Is this somebody that is going to submit to you and follow you? Does she admire you? Keep these things in mind. Make them the most important part of your list.

If your marriage has failed, can you see why... from both sides? Marriage is very simple.

GOD'S PART

God can do what you can't do. All you can do is obey the will of God. To love and to submit. The rest is up to Him. You can't make your husband or your wife more spiritual. You can't force them into a role that they don't want to fit into.

God has your best interest in heart. He can take your marriage and make you work as a team. He can take two and make them into one – forging them into a sword that is powerful against every work of the enemy!

Take your time through this final requirement for prophetic office. If the Lord has taken you on a detour to invest into your children or marriage, you are not alone!

I have seen the Lord do this time and again. Unfortunately, I have also seen some who tried to avoid this detour and shipwrecked their marriage and ministry. You need not fall into this category.

Rather go through the process now before you step over this threshold.

Before the Lord releases you into the fullness of your call, make sure that you are fully prepared to walk it out, and what a better way to do that, than someone who is devoted to you at your side, and your children supporting you from behind?

PART 02 – THE AUTHORITY OF PROPHETIC OFFICE

CHAPTER 08

CHARACTER OF PROPHETIC OFFICE

Part 02 – The Authority of Prophetic Office

Chapter 08 – Character of Prophetic Office

It is when you have worn a trail to Golgotha that you qualify for office, because it is only when you are hanging between heaven and earth that you realize the authority that God has given to you.

It is only when you stand in His power, covered by His blood, that you realize that you remain suspended, and Jesus gets off in your place.

Your ability to bring that flesh to the cross time and again means that you are a mighty commander in the hand of God that can be entrusted to always move forward. No matter what the enemy throws at you and no matter how much you fail, you know where your solution lies.

You realize that you are human and fleshly, but you know how to deal with that and get up again. Qualifying for prophetic office means coming to a knowledge of the poetry in this passage.

Matthew 5:3-10

3 Blessed are the poor in spirit, for theirs is the kingdom of heaven.
4 Blessed are those who mourn, for they shall be comforted.
5 Blessed are the meek, for they shall inherit the earth.
6 Blessed are those who hunger and thirst for righteousness, for they shall be filled.
7 Blessed are the merciful, for they shall obtain mercy.
8 Blessed are the pure in heart, for they shall see God.
9 Blessed are the peacemakers, for they shall be called sons of God.
10 Blessed are those who are persecuted for righteousness' sake, for theirs is the kingdom of heaven.

The prophet who is ready for office is easily identified because of how the journey has shaped them. Now not everyone responds the same way to the kinds of pressures that are faced in training, but perhaps this chapter will be a tremendous encouragement for you!

Up until this point, you have seen just the training and spiritual warfare, but you have not seen how much it has shaped you into the prophet that God always intended. In fact, we become so proficient in learning to "Die Already" that we often do not see the change that resurrection has brought about in our lives.

Do you remember in the first book *Prophetic Essentials*, I shared about all the signs of the prophet? Well as we bring this series to a close, I want to share some of the signs of someone who is ready for prophetic office. The Holy Spirit has been working and He has forged something wonderful out of the gold He has found in you!

THE CHARACTER OF PROPHETIC OFFICE

Based on Matthew 5, you are about to see how your life has become the principle that you have taught others for so long.

MOURN

The condition of the Church - the scattered debris of the battlefield you see each time you meet another believer does not leave you unchanged. You carry about in you, the mourning of Christ.

More times than you can count, you find yourself weeping in the presence of the Lord. Sometimes you are Moses interceding on their behalf. Sometimes you are Daniel trying to take on the sins of a nation.

> **KEY PRINCIPLE**
>
> The heart of the prophet is one that weeps. It is a heart that is so connected to that of the Lord Jesus that you feel His pain, anger, joy and passion for the Bride.

Yes, this has got you into trouble sometimes.

While everyone else wants to have a party, you feel an ache in your heart, looking at everything that is lacking. A lackluster Church that reminds you that they have forgotten their first love.

The mourning remains part of who you are. How you walk it out will change as you mature, but this one thing will always be yours – the bleeding heart of Jesus.

MEEK

One cannot face that much deception and failure, and still stand as a strong, arrogant tower. By the time you are ready for prophetic office, you are very, very far from admitting it to anyone.

The call of the prophet has become less of a title and more of a reality of the responsibility that is now placed on your shoulders.

Along with that revelation though, comes the realization that you are the person least capable of taking on that responsibility.

Your sin is in your face. Your flesh screams with all its nasty passions and self- promotion. It does not matter what anyone else tells you, because you know your own limitations.

You see the vastness of the call before you, and at the same time see your own inabilities. To say that you have come to understand His grace is an understatement. Instead, you declare in the quiet of your room, how you, the "chiefest of sinners" is the least qualified to lead the Church into this new land God has promised.

Brazen passion has been turned to a smoldering wick of humility - a wick that the Lord will never put out, but will bring back to fire again and again. This is where your power lies. Only someone who is ready for prophetic office understands that the power of God does not rest in arrogance, but in the meek heart of one who is well aware that God chose a weak vessel through which to show His glory.

> **KEY PRINCIPLE**
>
> The meeker you are, the greater He is. The greater your weakness, the greater His power.

The moment you lose the secret of meekness is the moment you step out of His power.

HUNGER AND THIRST

For so long, you sought after prophetic office as if it would meet the hunger and thirst in you. Yet as the Lord Jesus drew you to still waters and fed you honey by His hand, each taste stirred up a greater hunger in your soul.

The touch of His hand on your life and the anointing that saturates every part of your being stirs up yet more hunger. When you stop hungering, you stop ministering. When you stop thirsting, you stop walking forward.

Not only are you hungrier for Him now than before, you are keenly aware that it is this very thirst and hunger that propels you forward. You do not want to be full. You never want to say, "I have had enough of Jesus now."

Prophetic office does not have the power to satisfy your yearning within – only Jesus can do that. Not only has this season of training taught you how to have that need met, but has pointed you in the right direction.

The goal of prophetic office has given way now to Jesus who has His hand outstretched to you. You chase Him with your whole being, and you would not want it any other way. May the hunger deepen and your thirst propel you into His arms again and again!

Merciful

How can you judge when you know how much you have let Him down? You tried so hard! You tried to obey all the rules and... fell flat on your face every single time. You cannot do that nonstop for the process of at least 9 months and think that you are better than everyone else.

Nothing like a good look into your heart to have mercy for others. You might not like their sin any better, but you want to reach out to them and help them experience the same mercy that God has given to you.

You find that mercy draws men unto you where judgment had pushed them away before. Look at what just happened! You have begun to take on the merciful countenance of the Lord Jesus.

With each visit to the cross, you have taken on a piece of His heart and an aspect of his demeanor. When man looks at you, they can swear that for a moment there, they were not looking into your eyes, but instead saw Jesus there.

Through a hint of your smile and outstretched hand, they do not see your convictions, but the nature of the Lord shining through. Someone who sees past the dirt and their strong walls and offers mercy and a chance to get up again. How can you remain unchanged when you look back at what God has done in you?

How can you not want to give Him all you are and have? It is in moments like these, that you not only remember why you are on this road, but how much further you want to run for Him.

Pure in Heart

If you look up the word "pure" in the Strong's Concordance (g2513) one of the definitions says "to be refined by fire." To be cleansed with fire! That sums up your training to a tee! Your preconceived ideas and ambitions have been put through the fire so many times that you feel emptied out.

Have you ever wondered why the prophetic training process is one of being stripped? Perhaps by now you are beginning to understand. It has refined you. It has caused the gold in you to shine so brightly that you reflect the face of Jesus.

When you look at the Church with a heart refined by fire, you do not see your own ideas, but what God intends. You know as you are known. You see as He sees and begin to understand your place in the Church.

Peacemaker

Prophets are renowned as troublemakers! It gets us up in the morning! However, after all that fire you went through, you start seeing things with different eyes. Now, do not misunderstand me. You have not stopped being a troublemaker.

In fact, I would daresay that the devil knows your name and has a sentry standing watch just for you! However instead of seeing the Church being torn in two, you desire to see reconciliation.

Now that you are seeing things a bit more clearly, you are ready to admit that some of your convictions of the past were a tad misdirected! You needed a bit of balance. Some of the convictions were started by the Lord and then were added to in the flesh.

The fire sorted that out, and I am sure that as you look back now, you wish you could go back and repair some of the damage you have done through the years. Not to worry though, the Lord has your back and now is not the time to look back, but forward.

You will yet be used as His ambassador of peace!

FACING REJECTION AND REJOICING THEREIN

Sorry – training might be over, but rejection is still pretty much your friend. The difference? You *rock it*! Rejection no longer disables you, but is now the gas in your tank. Bring it on! When rejection comes, you know you are in the right place and you are ready to pick up the sword.

You know the voice of the enemy and when those words of accusation come at you, you know where the arrows were sent from. You no longer strive with flesh and blood, but know who is behind the attacks.

Now, I know of no true prophet that will lie down and willingly allow the devil to walk all over him! So yes…

when you realized that the rejection was the enemy's ace card against you, you cleaned him out and turned it against him.

Now when rejection comes, you roll with it so much you have to stop and think, "Yeah, that's right…. I just got a rejection, hey?" It became a way of life and no longer trips you up!

Guess what? You are well on your way to becoming a leader of influence! You are not afraid of the opposition and are ready to blaze a trail. Watch out Church!

BE PREPARED TO LET GO

It's true – if there is one thing that you have learned through your training it is how to let go! How to put your flesh on the cross, die to visions and let people go. In fact, you are so "cored out," you wonder what is left that God could possibly take.

You are in a good place, because it means that the Lord can take you anywhere He wants to take you! You are a soft piece of clay in His hands that He can shape again and again. Never stop being teachable and flexible in the hands of the Lord, because you will be shaped from glory to glory.

There will always be a new level to go to. Do not think that prophetic office is your goal. Prophetic office is the beginning of a journey. So prepare yourself for this journey.

Pack your ability to remain flexible. Make sure that you have enough mercy on you, and stockpile an abundance of meekness, because ready or not… office is on the way!

CHAPTER 09

THE PROPHET IN THE LOCAL CHURCH

Chapter 09 – The Prophet in the Local Church

Remember how all your ministry doors shut when you started your training? The Lord shook up your concept of ministry entirely. Good news! Things are about to change dramatically.

I already shared with you how the Lord begins to change your circumstances and one of the major shifts you will begin to experience as you enter office is how you operate in both the local and universal church!

So before pressing on, I want you to be very clear on what the difference is and what exactly what I mean by saying "local" or "universal" church! Time to pick up your pen and paper and make some notes.

> ***1 Corinthians 16:19*** *The churches of Asia greet you. Aquila and Priscilla greet you heartily in the Lord, with the church that is in their house.*

Do you see the two aspects of this scripture? We have the church in Asia and the church in the house. You see a local church and a universal church.

What I am going to focus on in this chapter, is the prophetic ministry in the local church. Everyone understands the concept of the prophetic ministry in the universal church. When I say, "You are called to the universal church" the picture is pretty clear.

You see the traveling evangelists and prophets, and you see the apostles going out and breaking new ground. However, we have yet to see what God is birthing right in front of us – the fivefold ministry in the local church.

When we have perfected it in the local church, we can then lead the Church of God into the glory that He has destined us for. However, we are jumping the gun. It is a progression.

Local Church

So then... what is the local church?

It is the place where people belong. It is where the body ministries and the fivefold ministry functions. It is a place with members of the body in it. It is a house - a home. There is a mom, a dad, and siblings. You have squabbles and fights, throw tantrums, and then love each other again the next day.

This is the local church. We need the local church. We need a mom and dad to rebel against and a sibling to argue with. We need to know that we can still come home and be loved.

I think you have a pretty good picture of what the local church looks like.

Universal Church

Now, the universal church is a very different picture. This is the Church as a collective group. It is like Paul was saying, "The Church in Asia."

When I say "universal", that word should immediately bring an image to mind. It is the Church of God, the body of Christ universally, in a state, a country, the world. It is the entire body of Christ as a whole.

MINISTRY VS. OFFICE

The fivefold offices will function in the universal church. I may throw a lot of new terms at you, but I want you to keep in mind the local church, universal church, fivefold ministry, and fivefold office. There is a progression.

I see a lot of confusion in the Church. You see someone that is clearly prophetic and you see that they are flowing as a prophet. Yet, you see another prophet and think, "They are kind of the same, but not entirely the same."

"One prophet goes out and he seems to have more authority. What is the difference? The functions seem similar, but what is the difference?"

The difference is between local and universal church, and the function of ministry and office. Perhaps God has told you that you need to move to prophetic office, so there is going to be a transition that you need to take.

Before you make that transition however, you need to have fulfilled your ministry in the local church first. You have to get your house in order. So as the Lord begins leading you into prophetic office, a lot is going to change.

Firstly, you are going to be led back to the local church. What?! You mean you just went through this gut wrenching "letting go" just to be sent back? Yes, prophet of God, you and Moses sing the same tune of, "But Lord I cannot! I cannot talk, I am not ready!"

Well how else did you think you were going to change the Church? By becoming like those traveling evangelists that go in, heal a few people, and leave?

Now I am not saying that you will not make that transition to reaching out beyond the local church, but until you have put your house in order, what do you have to come back home to?

Ah yes, everyone wants to "go out there." You want to reach office, not have a pastor to answer to, and just do your thing. Perhaps now is a good time to mention that you are just one of the fivefold ministry.

Do the math. You are one of five. If you head out all on your own, how on earth are you going to bring any change to the Church? So the Lord will lead you right to the one place where you will have the greatest impact... in the local church!

PROPHETIC MINISTRY IN THE LOCAL CHURCH

These were the good old days for you. Seen as though we are already going down memory lane, let me remind you of the birth of your prophetic ministry because soon the Lord will send you back to the local church to find other little prophets just like you – in the throes of preparation and trying to function in their ministry.

Perhaps because you have developed meekness, and are now merciful, you can extend the hand to them that you never received. Remember the old days? The bitter and the sweet moments that led you to this point in your life?

Look back with me and remember what someone in prophetic ministry looks like in a prophetic church!

EXHORTATION

You are going to see prophetic ministry in the local church as a ministry of exhortation. If you want to see prophetic ministry, just hang out with the intercessors before the meeting starts. There you will find prophetic ministry in action. (Triggering any memories yet?)

They bring people into a reality of Jesus (or at least should be anyway!).

The prophet says, "Get up off the chair and find your place in the body of Christ. Come on, let's get into a relationship with the Lord. Let's take hold of His power and do what He has called us to do!"

We need that.

PRAYER WARRIORS

These are the guys that are also laying the groundwork in prayer and have a passion for their community. When they are on their face before God, they are praying for the pastor, their home church, and their community.

They do not really pray beyond that. They are stuck right there. They try, but then it does not really work and they just go right back to praying for their community.

"Lord, I feel a bit bad. I should pray for more than just my city."

You try to move away from praying for your own city, however, you end up right back praying for your city again. This is prophetic ministry and we need more of it in the church.

People keep thinking, "If we can get more prophets to pray for our region, God is going to bring revival to our region. Let's get a prophet in office to come."

Come now! Can we just get enough prophets in the local church, in prophetic ministry, praying for their region? Then, we will see revival from within. We need to bring life from within the local church, not outside of it.

Our heart is within our chest, pumping blood to the rest of our body. That is how every organ is oxygenated. We do not breathe through our skin. However, we are trying to breathe through our skin in the body of Christ.

We keep bringing in people from the outside. Yes, there is a place for it, but when they are coming from the outside, should they not be breathing life on what is already on the inside?

Should it not encourage you to the next level as a body? Then, you can move forward.

THE ELISHAS AND SONS OF THE PROPHETS

Those that are functioning in prophetic ministry are going to be the Elishas. They are going to notice those that are functioning in the body ministry of prophecy. I call these ones, "sons of the prophets."

These are the ones that prophesy every now and again and get visions. These are the guys who you find yourself saying to, "You are kind of prophetic."

You do not want to say that they are a prophet because you see some aspects, but you really do not feel that they are fully prophets. I call people like this, the "sons of the prophets." Remember everything you learned about these types in the *Prophetic Boot Camp* book?

BUILDERS

> **KEY PRINCIPLE**
>
> Prophets in the local church function with the pastor, to build. Prophets are meant to be builders.

The evangelists are the ones that go and get the bricks. The teachers are the ones that help with the blueprint. The prophets are the ones that are meant to build. You would not think so with some of the prophets that I work with, but it is true.

Prophets are meant to be assisting the leadership in the church, so that they can build up the local church. Isn't that what the prophets did with Paul? Is that not what Silas did?

The Word said that they exhorted and they built up the people with many words.

"This is the direction that God is leading us in. Alright, what can I do? Who can I encourage? Where can I pray?"

That is why you will often see those in prophetic ministry up front with a microphone. What better way is there to bring people into a face-to-face relationship with Jesus than in praise and worship? Enter... *Prophetic Anointing*! I told you we were going on a walk down memory lane.

Releasing Body Ministries

The prophet in the local church will lay hands and release members into their body ministries and help identify their ministries.

They encourage God's people to press on and help them find their place. Then, they need to release the anointing on them to do it.

That is why I said that the prophet is one who helps the pastor build. The pastor will get the pattern. He will say, "This is the direction that we need to go in."

The prophet will say, "Pastor, the Lord has been giving me a revelation about this member. I really think that God is leading them in this direction."

He shares with the pastor and then he will release that on the person and ignite them.

They are not there to travel from church to church or stand up and prophesy all the time. That is the least of the prophetic ministry.

There comes a time when you will shift to office, but not everyone will. Some will remain as "sons of the prophets" and some will remain as Elishas. Then, there are some that God will call beyond the walls of their local church and into office.

Prophetic Office in the Local Church

They will then transition to Elijah. They will begin to get prayer burdens beyond their borders. They will start having doors open beyond their borders. They will begin to decree, release, plant, and uproot.

Prayer for Nations

Their intercession will start going to the nations. Their relationship will also change. Instead of working with the pastor, they will work with the apostle to build on a broader plane.

Now here is something that you need to think about - until you fulfill the function of prophetic ministry in the local church, you are not going to be ready for the universal church.

WORKING WITH THE APOSTLE

If you cannot even handle working with a pastor, how are you going to handle working with an apostle?

I know that I am not easy to work with and no apostle is because they know the refining fire and what God wants. They have gone through the deaths and they know how much God expects of them and they are going to expect the same thing from you.

If you cannot work with a pastor who nurtures and is the nice guy, then you are not going to make it under an apostle. So, make sure that you have fulfilled your function in the local church first.

Take all the tools that you need because I see a lot of prophets that have a hunger for God, but miss this step. They step out on their own, do not know how to relate to leadership, and it does not go well for them.

The Lord has to bring them a team, arrange circumstances, but they bounce from place to place. I have seen so much heartbreak and hurt. They are alone and lonely.

Let me tell you something. As a prophet in office, you will experience so much warfare. You are attacked by the hordes of hell. The princes of the air come against you and you need somebody at your back.

However, if you have not learned that in the local church, how are you going to do it in the universal?

As a mom, I would like to think that I have raised my girls to be prepared for the world out there. I have taught them about heartache and I have taught them how to wear high heels. I have taught my son to be a gentleman and a protector.

I have given them all the secrets for becoming a success out there, by giving them a place to practice all those things in a safe, home environment. They are going to face the winds and waves out there, but I would like to think that I have raised them well enough to weather those storms.

Are you strong enough to weather the storms in the universal church? Are you strong enough to weather the princes of an entire country?

You think that you are battling with the little prince in your local church and town. What do you think that you are going to face out there, when you are taking on a nation?

Take time to grow. Don't skip any steps because God has a plan and a pattern. Just as He gave it to Moses and David, He is very specific.

Make sure that you are perfected before you begin to build. You need to reach full maturity so that God can rely on you.

READY AND SET?

You are waiting for God to send you out. However, are you ready? Have you grown up at home yet?

I do not care if your pastor is the most dominating person in the world. There are things that you can learn in here that trust me… you do *not* want to learn out there. If you think this rejection is bad, wait until satan has his hand on you. Then, we can talk again about rejection.

Get strong. Become like John the Baptist and wax strong in the wilderness. Then when you rise up, people will say, "Wow. You just rose up overnight. You are so strong."

You will say, "You have no idea! I had to eat locusts under that pastor, brother. Do you know what he made me wear? We are talking burlap, here!"

You have no idea how many treasures you have taken from that time. Yes, I know that when you look back at where you have come from, there are still some splinters in your heart that prick you from time to time.

There is something you should know though. You are not the same person anymore. You have changed! You have grown and the Lord has put His heart into you. You need not be afraid to face that pastor again, because this time you will be the one too happy to eat wild honey and wear burlap!

God has a work for you to do right now, so get ready for it, because the doors are about to open.

CHAPTER **10**

NAVIGATING THE LOCAL CHURCH RULES

Chapter 10 – Navigating The Local Church Rules

So, here I am once again, to give you the insider information that will save face time and again! Ok, so you have come to the realization that God is sending you back… but how? The set of rules you went by the last time did not work out very well.

Those rules lead to the wilderness, many visits to the cross, and the odd leg-breaking experience. Can we please be past these dramatic turn of events at this stage of your calling? Well, gather round and take notes, because there really is an easy way.

I am going to lay out the rules for you nicely and clearly, so that there will not be any excuses or misunderstandings.

Rule #1 Administrative Order

If you have done any study on the office of pastor, you will discover something fascinating – the function of the pastor is twofold. In fact, I suggest you brush up a little bit on the pastor's function in the *Today's Pastor* book to give you some perspective.

We are all familiar with the ministry aspect that the pastor should be fulfilling, but his is also an administrative appointment. A leadership position whereby he is given the care of the church.

Now he might not get all the revelation or even see as you see, but here is the truth... he is the leader in the local church. This is his home and he is a very grumpy mama bear if someone comes around messing with his cubs.

> ### *Key Principle*
>
> Once you understand that the fire you have for ministry is very different from the fire that a pastor has, you will begin to find your place and work together.

Now every church has their own established administration and here is not the place for me to go into what I think the perfect structure is!

The reality is... you need to change the Church. You need to bring the bride of Christ into a relationship with Him. That means working with what you have. What you have right now is a local church that might not even be open to the gifts of the Spirit! What do you do?

You remember that there is an order of things. Consider this passage:

> ***Romans 13:1*** *Let every soul be subject to the governing authorities. For there is no authority except from God, and the authorities that exist are appointed by God*

We are talking about administration here. I am not telling you to let go of your convictions or the words of decree that God has told you to give. I am teaching you how to play well with others!

The first step towards that is knowing your place and becoming comfortable with it. I have seen prophets take their place in the church, and as they are given more liberty, bring massive change to the congregation.

The problem is, you want the Church to change right now! You have not been prepared to begin where they are and lead them at a pace that is good for them. You want the leadership to just "get the revelation" instead of proving yourself and gaining respect first, by learning to follow.

Establish Your Pulpit

Yes, you might even have been placed in prophetic office, but what use is all that spiritual authority if you do not have any liberty to use it? So go to where God sends you and walk through the open doors that you are given!

Have you been given leadership of the intercessory team? Then you have your pulpit. Have you been given charge of a cell group or some kind of committee? Then you have the open door you need to become an influence.

Operate in all the functions of the prophet God has given to you, within this realm. Do not try to function as that prophet in a pulpit that you have not been given... I promise... you will fall flat on your face.

Rather fulfill your purpose in the position that you do have and begin to build with the pastor. You cannot force the leadership to do things your way – no matter how many revelations you have. What you can do though is be a little leaven! Think about it! If the enemy can spread deception through someone he has bound, why can't the Holy Spirit use you to spread a fire of revival in the Church?

> **KEY PRINCIPLE**
>
> So to clarify – you can only preach in the pulpits you are given. You cannot appoint yourself to a pulpit.

If you try to do that, you will find yourself knocked off it for good. So find your place in the local church. What opportunities have you been given? Find your place of peace in that administrative order and then... let the prophet in you loose in that realm!

You prophesy, decree, intercede, build up, exhort and change the church from within!

A LEADERSHIP TIP

Here is another little tip from one who has both followed and led. If the Lord opens the door for you to participate in a ministry or local church, do not be afraid to ask the leader there what they expect of you.

Allow them to establish your boundaries and to know what you both expect. Communication is the best policy. You can ask questions like,

"Are you open to prophesying in the public meeting?"

"Are you open for me to teach the intercessors to pray using petition as well as prophetic decree?"

By keeping communications open, you begin building with the leadership and not apart from them. Not only that, but you have backing! They know you are at their backs and you know they will back you too if anyone gives you a tough time. Come now… look at how much you have changed! You can do this!

Rule #2 Meeting Order

This follows on perfectly from what I just shared. It is essential that you know what the established meeting order is. Now I am not saying you will like it… I am saying you need to know what it is, if you are going to be effective!

God is a God of order. You must abide by the order of the public meeting, but there is this one purpose that will remain… you will always use exhortation and encouragement as part of your ministry.

So let's look at that meeting order. For example, if you are given the liberty to share in the public meeting and

God gives you a word, then sure, you can share it. However, if they forbid the sharing of words in public meetings, you cannot rebel against that authority.

Yes… it's wrong! It is even against the word. Think about this though – if the Church was perfect, would God need to send you? Your very ministry is proof of the fact that the Church isn't where it is meant to be. So do not expect perfection and stop getting frustrated that everyone does not see things correctly (as you see it).

You are being sent, because things aren't right! If it was perfect – what would God need you for?

So start with where they are at, and keep praying for God to move.

You see, the leader of that church is responsible for the public meeting and how they run their ministry. Unless it is your meeting, you have to abide by the guidelines. This will bring a lot of peace to the body of Christ because we have lots of prophets coming with their contradictory ideas all jumping up and wanting to do things their way.

It is chaos. God is a God of order.

Here is some hope though… your prophetic authority will stand whether they receive what you have to say or not.

Isn't that the best part? Isn't that what we are trying to accomplish here? Unity and change in the Church? So does it matter if their structure is what you agree with? Does it matter whether or not they believe in prophets?

I am about to give you another "insider secret."

I was asked by someone what to do when God sent them to a church that did not believe in prophets. Firstly, I have to respond with, "So? Are you going there to be a prophet, or are you going there to minister to God's people?"

So firstly… put the office down. Secondly, ask God, what He wants to say.

Do you know that you can give a prophetic word in such a way that it sounds like you are just sharing words of inspiration? You need not throw "thus saith the Lord" out every second sentence. You also do not need to get all emotional and throw yourself into a dramatic fit.

Rule #3 Find the Right Approach

I have seen God leading prophets to attend Catholic, Anglican, and Baptist churches. You are thinking, "Lord, what am I doing here?"

They were sent to speak God's word and to decree His will so that it might come to pass. They do not even get an opportunity to minister in the meetings.

God sent them there for one purpose and that is to make sure that God's will was fulfilled in that church.

You are quite capable of standing in front of a congregation that does not believe in any of the gifts of the Spirit and speak under the inspired power of God. You are well able to share from a perspective whereby you are giving them a prophetic word, but they really do not know it.

Hmmm, let me see if I can clarify. Say for example you receive the following words from the Lord,

"My children, my arms are reached out to you. Run to me now and I will heal the hurts of your heart. For I have seen what has happened to you and I know that you feel alone, but now it is time to set your sin aside and come into my presence…"

Ok, so now you are standing in a church that does not agree with prophecy and is dead against those flaky "prophetic types." You are in the perfect place, if you ask me, because this church needs the prophetic ministry more than anyone else!

Are you going to stand up and walk out, or share Jesus' heart with them? So come now prophet, pick up the lessons that you learned on tact in the *Prophetic Functions* book and share that same word… but like this:

"The Lord's arms are always reached out to you. All you need to do is run to Him and He will heal you. The Lord has seen the things that have happened to you and He came to heal the broken-hearted. I know, that if we as a Church are prepared to lay our sin down and go to the

Lord, that He is standing there to bring the healing we need. Healing that is only found in His presence… "

It's all about delivery. What many leaders find offensive about prophetic ministry is not that they are speaking for God, but rather *how* they are speaking for God. They are uncomfortable with the showmanship and uncontrollable spasms and head flinging that has become so popular in this day and age.

The sad truth though, is that it is the churches that are the deadest that need this move of the Spirit the most! However, prophets flock to churches open to prophetic ministry and gifts of the Spirit. Do not douse your fire.

Do not stop being the prophet God has called you to be. Keep your passion, hunger, mourning, and hours of crying out to God in the night. Then step into the local church and present to them, a Jesus that they understand!

When Jesus was with Nicodemus, He spoke His language. He spoke differently to the woman at the well. He reached each one where they were at and from there, led them to truth. It is your mandate to do the same.

So let's learn, in a book about prophetic office, how vital it is to lay down the title of prophetic office!

You see, whether they run the meeting God's way or not, it does not change who you are and you do not have to feel threatened by it.

You do not have to judge either. You can just go and be available to exhort. So, do not be surprised if you do not get to function in the fullness of office in a public meeting. You can function in the prophetic gifts and in prophetic ministry.

BALANCING ADMINISTRATION AND MINISTRY

You see, prophet, administrative authority and spiritual authority are two very different things. As far as God is concerned, you speak the word that needs to be spoken, and you decree His will. You do not need the approval of man for that.

Yet, as far as administrative authority is concerned, each one must have their place. If the administrative authority gives you license to function in that local church, you may only function in the capacity that they allow.

The rest of the work that you do, will be done outside of the local church in the body of Christ universal. As you enter into prophetic office, you are going to find that your function in the local church is not going to be as much as you did before.

In fact, because you are in prophetic office, you should be stepping back and allowing those that are in prophetic ministry to step forward. You should be the more mature one who sits down and allows the younger prophets to come up and share. You should be the one who is a source of hope and encouragement to those starting out.

Ah yes, wouldn't that have been nice when you were there? To just have someone to let you know you were not crazy? Someone to help speak healing to your heart? This journey of yours has forged more in you than you know.

I want to end off with some fun ideas of how you can function practically in your local church. Taking everything you have learned so far, here are some skills you have to offer any leader who wants you to help build the Kingdom of God!

1. Instruction on dream interpretation
2. Teach the intercessory group how to pray
3. Instruction on how to journal
4. To lead worship and bring the presence of the Lord Jesus into the meetings
5. To help identify people's body ministries
6. To exhort through the gift of prophesy
7. Teach on how to hear the voice of God
8. You can preach, pray and worship!
9. Minister to hurts of the past
10. Making the church battle ready! Practical training on how to overcome curses. (Remember *Prophetic Warrior* and *Prophetic Counter Insurgence*?)

These are just a few off the top of my head. You have more to offer than you realize. Now it is time for you to mentor and impart that knowledge to others. You need to teach believers to hear God for themselves. Teach those in prophetic ministry how to pray correctly.

You should even be mentoring other prophets and helping them identify their callings. These are all functions that you should be fulfilling in the local church, if the local church you are in, permits you to do so.

If not, and God directs you to do so, find another local church, but do not try to change the leadership. If God leads you out of a ministry, make sure that you leave good fruit behind. Can you look back and see the lives you invested in?

They might not have been ready for the full truth, but did you give them what they *were* ready for? If so, you have started a process that the Holy Spirit will continue to develop. Like I said before, you are just one of the fivefold – what you have begun, another of the fivefold will finish. You just became part of something much bigger than yourself. Good, you are well on your way to making an impact as a prophet to the Church.

CHAPTER 11

THE PROPHET IN THE UNIVERSAL CHURCH

CHAPTER 11 – THE PROPHET IN THE UNIVERSAL CHURCH

The day you enter prophetic office is the day you begin to feel a shift in your calling. Not only will you feel the increase in authority, but your spiritual eyesight will be extended beyond your borders.

Where before you felt a passion and call to pray for your local church or ministry, suddenly you will find the Holy Spirit lifting the veil to the rest of the Church. You will begin to travail and weep for those you have never met before.

You have just stepped beyond the Jordan River and find yourself facing a whole new ballgame. We are quick to look at the excitement of "going over the Jordan," but no one remembers what came next.

First, Joshua had a "circumcision party" up on Foreskin Hill. This was followed by a seven-day march around Jericho. That still… was just the beginning. From there the real work began. After dreaming about what the Promised Land would look like, the Israelites could start to take hold of that land. Keep this in mind though – it was not just handed to them.

They had to fight for every square inch of it! Do you remember in *Prophetic Warrior* how I took your hand through all that spiritual warfare? If ever you are going to need it, it is the day you are placed in prophetic office.

Well what did you think that prophetic authority was for? Just to show it off? No, with the increased authority, comes a call to take the land on behalf of God's people. Do you think that Joshua was taking the land for his own gain?

The man was old! He could well have settled on the other side of the Jordan and lived out his golden years in peace. Yet at the striking age at of ninety, he decided to pick up his sword and spend the last of his twenty years fighting his heart out!

Seems crazy doesn't it? Well, what did you think all this training was for? It is to walk it out! Suddenly you come to realize that reaching prophetic office was not about your calling.

> **KEY PRINCIPLE**
>
> Reaching prophetic office is about the Church's calling in this world. You have been anointed to win back the land for God's people – not yourself.

Now when you pick up that sword, a few things are going to change.

Firstly, the Lord will ensure that you get your home in order. He will have you wrap up everything in the local church. From there, a shift will begin to take place.

Either you will rise up in leadership in that local church, or eventually help build it with the apostle. This is not the case for everyone. For some, their Moses "dies" and they take over.

Yet, there others that are a bit like Caleb. Although he was submitted completely to Joshua, he did not sit around to wait for his land to come to him! He picked up his own sword (at the tender age of ninety) and took the land for himself!

This is what it looks like to transition to the universal church. Before I give you an outline of what your place is though, let's have a quick summary of what the universal church actually is.

From there, we can look at the part you should be playing in it.

THE UNIVERSAL CHURCH PERSONALITY

Firstly, it is a place where large gatherings take place. Here you will find a variety of callings, passions, and interests. Where the local church usually centers around a specific purpose, these public meetings will reach every kind of believer with every kind of passion.

It says in Acts 2:46 that they continued daily with one mind in the temple and they broke bread from house to house and ate their food with gladness.

They had these two aspects. They had the breaking of bread from house to house and they had the temple where they all met from all the local churches. You have your family church, and you have the universal church where believers from every walk of life gather.

One is public and one is personal.

1. Public Meetings

The function of the universal church includes public meetings, preaching, and getting the leaders together to tell them what they should be doing and teaching God's people.

From there, leaders can go and filter it down to their local churches.

2. Being Sent Out

Functioning in the universal church involves being sent out. In each instance, the apostles and prophets were sent out to reach unchartered territory (Paul and Barnabas a classic example).

In cases where there are lots of believers, like in Samaria, apostles were sent to go and lay hands on them so that they could receive the Holy Spirit and then get the organization set up and everything put into place.

3. To Establish Structure

The apostles did not stay there though. Apostle Paul told Timothy and Titus to go and appoint elders in every city.

He did not tell them to go and play church. He told them to appoint elders and get the members together.

Working with the universal church means helping local churches find structure and discover what kind of organ they are in the Body. Once again, depending on the kind of fivefold minister you are, how you will accomplish this will differ.

4. Distribution

It says in Acts that everyone came and laid everything at the apostles' feet. They gave all the finances to the apostles at each headquarter, and from there it was distributed to those that had need. Working in the universal church involves distributing between members so that everyone is blessed.

This relates to financial and spiritual things!

Your Transition to the Universal Church

Are you beginning to understand why you had to qualify in the local church first? How can God trust you with a word that influences multiple churches, when you have not qualified yet to do it in one?

Get your own house in order first. Then qualify to give direction to the homes of others! Now the emphasis I want to place on you right now, is that you are not alone. I have mentioned the fivefold ministry a lot and you are going to hear even more of it.

As the Lord transitions you to the universal church, there are a couple of things that you need to take into account.

1. Local Church Involvement Shifts

Now if the Lord is about to send you out to reach more ministries, your home life is going to change. Now is a good time to ask yourself whether you have fulfilled your purpose in that local church.

Have you taught God's people to hear Him for themselves? In addition to that, have you trained up another leader to take your place? You cannot just walk out, without leaving a support system behind.

What is the point of investing so much work into a ministry and then leaving it like you found it? The purpose of your ministry is to bring that ministry to a new level of maturity. Have you accomplished that?

Unfortunately, I have seen so many prophets receive the call to the universal church and simply dump their responsibilities at home. In the end, that ministry is in a worse state than when they entered it! What is the use of the Lord sending you to a ministry that you leave in pieces? Unless that was His intention, you have not done your job correctly.

So make sure you tie up those loose ends because change is coming. Your relationships are going to change. Where before you related to a pastor or ministry leader, you will now begin working with an apostle. This alone will bring a major shift in your calling. It means letting go of the daily running of the local church or ministry you are involved in.

Do your best. Invest all you can into the person who is taking over and then… let it go! By all means continue fellowship and remain a source of encouragement for that church, but above all… let go! You cannot have your cake and eat it.

You cannot continue to invest the same amount of effort into that ministry and still build where God wants you to build. It's time to move. Let go of the relationships, and put the future growth of that work into His hands. He is a pretty big God… I am sure He can make up for the slack you leave behind!

2. Vision Will Change

Until this point, your vision has been focused locally. It is about to change. This change will likely begin to happen during your times of intercession. You will start to see things beyond your borders. You will start to get a passion beyond what your local ministry is doing.

You will become restless. It is at this point that conflict has a perfect breeding ground – especially if you do not realize what is going on! You will start to feel stifled and frustrated with the leadership there. You will feel to move in a new direction and they will dig in their heels. You feel that God wants to expand them, but they are not catching the vision!

There is a reason for this – this is your vision – it is not theirs! Let it go. Transition is coming and you need to allow the Holy Spirit to expand that vision. You need to see beyond the borders of the position and responsibility you had.

Isn't that encouraging though? It means that you are about to pick up your sword and take the land.

3. Circumstances Shift Dramatically

This can be confusing if you do not see what God is doing. Here is something you really need to take into account. If God has called you to minister to the universal church, it stands to reason that you cannot stay at home!

It means that your feet have to get moving and this means physically as well as spiritually! It means that you are about to move house, or in some cases, sell your house and head out into the great unknown!

So before you think that you are "called to the nations" realize that to go to the nations, you have to well… go *out*!

Key Principle

> You cannot reach the world from your couch. It means going beyond your borders and leaving home.

So expect a dramatic shift of your circumstances. You might get fired from your job, or put in for a transfer. The Lord might have someone knock on your door who is international. Either way, do not get comfortable with your sofa because it is about to go!

4. Ministry Gifts Increase

"YES! I am finally in prophetic office! YES! I am finally being sent out to the nations and God has just told me that I must become... a pastor?!?!"

Get ready for it, because it's coming. You went through all this training and death to become a prophet, only for the Lord to call you to be a pastor or to teach. Does that make any sense at all?

Come now, how many times do I have to try and separate your office from your function? Your office will give that authority, but there is a lot more to do in the Church than praying and giving prophetic words.

To help people find their place, you will need to teach at times. I have seen so many prophets fail right at this very point! They just want to keep "flowing in the revelation gifts" and feeling all the power and do not take it a step further to learn to teach properly.

For many though, I have seen the Lord lead someone who just made it to prophetic office, to pastor. Why the sudden shift? In the book, *Prophetic Mandate*, you will learn how the first thing you go through after you reach office, is leadership training. There is no way to be a better leader than to become a pastor.

Not only that, but you are going to need the nurturing nature of the pastor to balance out the intensity of the prophetic sword you have. You need a balance to make sure that you fulfill your purpose. So if God starts leading you in this direction, stop spitting and spewing and get on with the program. The Church needs some building, and to do that building, you need the pastoral edge you are missing.

5. Your Reach Increases

It stands to reason that if your ministry gifts are expanding, that your ministry influence will as well. For those who are "prophets all the way" they will only draw the same kind of person to themselves.

They will draw the "black and white" believers who are straight as an arrow. They will draw those that appreciate their intensity. The problem with this, is that you limit the kind of influence you have in the Church.

So as the Lord starts to stretch you into some of the other ministry functions, you will reach more people. Learning to be a pastor will smooth over your rough edges and attract those that need the nurturing you can now offer them.

Now I am not saying that you will reach each office of the fivefold, but you will most certainly have a taste of each. In my teaching, *The Fivefold Offices for Today* you will see the progression that every minister goes through – you included!

New doors will open. You will reach people of different denominations and cultures. You cannot stay at home for that. You can rest assured that if the Lord has called you to step out, where you are standing right now is not where you will be standing next year.

So my advice to you is this: stop fighting and stop trying to make it come to pass according to your own terms. Stop giving God a "yes… but," and roll with it. Hand over all those things you have accumulated through the years. Let go of your house, car and relationships that you would "die without" and let God take over.

I am going to end with a stern warning.

> **KEY PRINCIPLE**
>
> As God calls you to the universal church, you will have a greater responsibility. More will be required of you. Your mistakes will now effect more people, so the fire will increase also.

If you mean business with God, then be prepared to let go of what you consider to be comfortable. Your job, house, money and comfort zone. Now, not every prophet in office is called to this, however if you are, you cannot take this step on your own terms. It has to be God's way or no way.

This call comes with a greater call to the cross, a greater price of responsibility, and as Apostle Paul said, "always bearing about in the body the dying of the Lord Jesus..." (2 Corinthians 4:10) Still feel that call? Then face the road ahead of you with confidence, for with everything you let go, you can be sure the Lord will return to you. You are embarking on the journey of a lifetime.

CHAPTER 12

THE PROPHETIC KEY

Chapter 12 – The Prophetic Key

> *Matthew 16:19 And I will give you the keys of the kingdom of heaven, and whatever you bind on earth will be bound in heaven, and whatever you loose on earth will be loosed in heaven.*

When the Lord first started leading us to release someone into prophetic training, we kept seeing this golden key in the Spirit. Not quite sure what that was, we released it by faith. It did not take us long to realize what was going on, because not long after receiving that key, the person in question would start going through the fire.

It was through this simple process of just being obedient and taking notes, that we came to understand the concept of prophetic training as I laid it out in *Prophetic Boot Camp*. Through the years, the Lord started to teach me what this key was and the vital part it plays in the life of the prophet.

I have spoken extensively about the authority that the prophet carries. This key is a symbol of that authority. There is no better scripture that describes it than the one found in Jeremiah.

> *Jeremiah 1:10 See, I have this day set you over the nations and over the kingdoms, to root out and to pull down, to destroy and to throw down, to build and to plant."*

ANOINTING VS. AUTHORITY

From the time the Lord starts you on your prophetic journey, the goal is simple. To fulfill your purpose in the Church. To fulfill that purpose though, you need some authority.

So take a little time to separate the difference between the anointing and authority here. The anointing is the proof of the Holy Spirit moving on the earth. If you will, it is the touch of the Holy Spirit. It is His caress, making you aware of His presence. You feel it tangibly.

Here is what you need to understand though – it takes authority to give the Holy Spirit license to move!

It's like this – when you speak in authority, the Holy Spirit moves!

Now various ministry leaders will operate in a different anointing, however regardless of the fruit of that anointing, authority is required!

> **KEY PRINCIPLE**
>
> Authority is not a feeling. Authority is not something that you can "work up." You either have it or you do not.

Remember the sons of Sceva trying to cast out demons? They did not have the authority and got beaten up!

Then you have Jesus who could stand up and tell the winds and waves to cease. Take an even closer look at this passage:

> **Matthew 10:1** *And when He had called His twelve disciples to Him, He gave them power over unclean spirits, to cast them out, and to heal all kinds of sickness and all kinds of disease.*

See what this passage says? He gave them power! He gave them authority. It does not say that He gave them the anointing to cast demons out. I will tell you this though, when they spoke, there is no doubt in my mind that the person they prayed for, felt the Holy Spirit!

WHY A KEY?

There are many symbols that I see with regards to the prophetic ministry. When I am praying for someone, I might see a harp in the spirit. When I do, I know the Lord wants them to flow in psalmody. When I see a trumpet, I know He wants them to operate in decree.

When I see a jar of oil, I know that He wants them to minister in inner healing. So when I see a key, I know that the Lord wants to train this person to operate in prophetic authority.

He is extending the opportunity to them, to qualify to receive some of His authority in the earth. So why a key? That is also what I wondered and sought the Lord and the Word. The more He led me, the more it was clear. When you look in Scriptures, you will see how a key speaks of spiritual authority! To have a "key" means to have authority in this earth!

> **Revelation 3:8** *I know your works. See, I have set before you an open door, and no one can shut it…*

Until now, you have looked in great detail at the operation and purpose of the prophet, but now you are about to understand something so much deeper. You are about to take hold of the authority of the prophet. That is what the prophetic key is all about.

When the gifts are gone and the show is over… what remains? When the prophetic gifts have ended and you have preached what you needed to, what fruit will you leave behind? Let me tell you, whether that word will come to pass or not depends on the authority you have.

Remember when I taught you about decree in the *Prophetic Anointing* book? I spoke about how you needed to increase your faith. Suddenly, what you have gone through in your training will make a full picture.

There is a reason that you faced those financial struggles. There was a reason that you faced those relationship frustrations. When you were released into prophetic training, the Lord handed you a key and said, "Come, let me teach you how to use it!"

Preparation ended, training began, and from that day onward, you started to qualify to receive the authority of prophetic office.

PROPHETIC MINISTRY VS. PROPHETIC OFFICE

In prophetic ministry, you received the gifts of the spirit and were given a direction. You began to "play around" with this new found authority. It is as if the Lord gave you a small piece of His authority to test you out!

Each time you got caught up in bitterness, you felt the anointing wane. When you walked in disobedience, the revelations ceased or you got into deception! Slowly, you began to qualify.

You learned that being a prophet was less about the gifts and more about *becoming the gift* to the Church you were called to be.

Without realizing it, you have been learning to use this authority in a secure environment. Is it any surprise then, that the Lord has had to take some prophets out of their church to let them learn? Too often they are like children, using this newfound authority the wrong way! Instead of building up, they tear down.

So for your (and the Church's) sake, the Lord takes you into isolation so that you can flip the switch of this nuke without taking out half the neighborhood! As your training comes to an end though, it is a time of reckoning.

Have you qualified to have the full authority of a prophet? Because once you receive it, there is no undoing it. Ever wonder how some of the greats of the past, like William Branham, who clearly got into deception, still flowed mightily in the anointing?

He walked in the authority that was given to him, regardless of his righteousness. Let that thought sink in a bit, would you? Would you give a child a loaded gun? Well, neither would God, and that is why you were given that little key, on loan, to qualify!

Because once you are given full prophetic authority, you have been given "license to kill". You better be sure that you are taking out the works of the enemy and not half of the Church every time you have a flip out over being rejected!

This authority is the foundation of your calling. It is the power in your times of intercession and the secret to releasing the anointing through praise and worship. It is what ensures that the words you speak do not return to you void and so that the decrees you issue come to pass.

Speak a "spot on word" without any authority and… nothing will happen! Speak half a word out with authority and it will surely come to pass! All the stripping and changing you have been through, is qualifying you.

As you stand today, tell me, do you qualify for this authority? Once it is in your hand, can the Lord trust that what you speak will do what He intends and not what you intend?

It's simple. Think about the words you throw out at random. Do you realize that they hold power? What is going to happen when that power increases? If you cannot control your tongue right now, then how will you control it when you have greater authority?

If you cannot handle a peashooter, what on earth are you going to do with a bazooka? This is what your training process has been about. Bit by bit, the Lord is bringing everything into line. Your family, marriage, circumstances, and your flesh. All must be brought into obedience. As a prophet, you will have authority to build up, tear down, uproot, and plant.

> **KEY PRINCIPLE**
>
> You cannot take a word back that has been spoken forth in authority.

You better be sure then, that you speak what God wants you to speak and are not still full of your own ideas and fleshly desires.

RESPONSIBILITY

You are about to discover that there is more to being a prophet than just saying the right words and flowing in all the gifts. In fact, you can flow in all of the spiritual gifts, you can even fulfill a prophetic mandate, but, until you have that prophetic authority, you are not in prophetic office.

Until you have that prophetic authority, you are not bringing any change. It reminds me of when my eldest daughter got the keys to her first car. She still had her learner's license and there was more than one hair-raising moment sitting in the passenger seat as she learned to drive. (And every parent out there, passes me a sympathetic smile...)

You see, until you learn to handle this ministry vehicle - until you learn to handle the curves in the road, the dips and the dives, and everything else that comes along, you are not ready to drive this car.

You know what it is like to transition from prophetic ministry to prophetic office? It is like this: Up until now, you have ridden a nice little mini Cooper and suddenly you get into this huge big Suburban van - one of those nice big, chunky American cars.

You are not riding in your little Mini anymore. You are now driving in the big town, on the big highways, with the big cars. It reminds me of the day my daughter finally got her license and braved the six lane freeways in San Diego after only driving mostly in the suburbs! It is time to run with the big boys now. With prophetic office comes a lot more responsibility, and with it comes prophetic authority.

It takes a greater authority, and it takes a greater responsibility. That is what the prophetic key is all about.

This authority I am talking about supersedes knowing what a prophet is. This means standing in the official appointment and authority of office.

FUNCTIONS OF THE PROPHETIC KEY

Let's have a look at what this prophetic key does. You will find a lot of that when the Lord spoke to Jeremiah and said, "See I have this day set you over the nations and over kingdoms, to root out and to pull down, to destroy and to throw down, and to build and to plant."

That's some responsibility, isn't it? You see, that is the authority of the prophet. To be able to pull down and to destroy. But, also to build up and to plant. To close doors on behalf of others, and to open doors on behalf of others.

When Jeremiah spoke those words and when the prophets spoke those decrees with that prophetic authority it didn't matter that the kings didn't like what they had to say. It didn't matter that the kings disagreed, that they burnt their scrolls and said, "No, I don't want to receive that word."

It didn't matter. Guess what? It still came to pass. That is the authority of the prophet.

THINGS HAPPEN

When you send out a prophetic word under the anointing of the Lord, with that authority, that word will accomplish that for which it was sent. When you send a word that opens a door on behalf of somebody else, that door will be opened, regardless of whether they understand the door, see the door, want the door, or know the door. It doesn't matter. You spoke it forth, so it is going to happen.

That is the kind of authority that the prophetic key holds.

It is also the kind of authority that when the Lord says, "I want that relationship severed" that when you sever it - it is gone. It is the kind of authority that says, "I want that church torn down" and when you speak it, it is gone.

That when the Lord wants you to release this person and put them here, in the spirit, when you do it, it is done whether they like it or not.

When Samuel came to Saul and said, "That is it, God has given your kingdom to another." There wasn't a "maybe," there wasn't a "Oh well, perhaps the Lord will change his mind," or "Perhaps there is something you can do about it, Saul." It was over, it was decreed, and it was gone.

And it was so as God said and Samuel declared it. As Samuel looked at Saul and said, "God has given your kingdom to another, a man after His own heart," that day, it was done. We know the story. David rose up to be the greatest king that ever lived.

Understanding Training

That is what we are talking about. Can you see why you need to come to a place of maturity? Why you need a phase of preparation, and then of training to get that job done? Because you are going to be messing with people's lives. God cannot trust you to go tearing down, building, planting, and to give you that authority when you are doing it with your own motivation and your sinful fleshly intentions.

That is why the preparation and training is so intense. This authority is something that you are going to start recognizing in your own life and in the lives of others.

Measure them by Their Words

There are many prophets that stand up with their revelations of "the Lord is going to give you the anointing for warfare."

"The Lord says that you are going to write a book."

"The Lord said that you are going to get married next year this time." Sometimes, I get exhausted listening to those guys.

Follow them up. Follow their word up. Does it come to pass? Did that person really enter into what that prophet said? Did those doors really open or didn't they?

The scripture is clear. It says in the Old Testament that if you want to see if somebody is a prophet, see if their word comes to pass. They were known as a prophet because every word they gave came to pass.

Why? Because they could hear God more clearly? No, there were many others that could also hear the voice of God. Even Saul could prophesy.

What made Samuel different? It was the authority with which he spoke. When he sent a word out, Scripture says that not a word he spoke fell to the ground. Now that is prophetic authority!

You will know that you have it when you speak and that word comes to pass. It is no longer a "for your interest, the Lord just wants you to know..." It is not that kind of word at all.

You declare, you release, and you speak forth into people's lives. It is the kind of authority that when I pray for somebody and release the gifts in them, they start manifesting those gifts immediately.

When I impart the gift of discerning of spirits to someone and they receive it, they have it immediately. That when I, in the spirit, break a tie, it is broken.

That when I, in the spirit, open the door on behalf of somebody else, that door opens.

That when the Lord says to me, "I want that relationship severed with these people," when I speak it, it gets severed. It happens. When the Lord says, "Something is going on there. I want you to expose the darkness" and I speak it forth, it gets exposed. You come to a place of expecting it to happen.

Can you see why you had to go through this process of learning to walk in faith? As a prophet, we forget that sometimes. We forget that it is not our authority, that it is not our ability to prophesy. It is knowing what God wants and simply decreeing His will into the earth.

Speaking His Will Into the Earth

It is not about babbling what you think or feel, but decreeing what you know God has given you to decree in this earth. If you stop for a moment, get away from all the "touchy-feely" stuff, and just listen to His voice about what He wants. Put yourself in a position of being used of Him to decree, and we are going to see a change in the body of Christ and in the world universal as we have never seen it.

If the prophets would just stand up in the fullness of authority, they could tear down kingdoms and build up other kingdoms. They could change the economy. They could change the Church.

We have that authority. If we just wait on the Lord and on what He has to say, what He wants in that circumstance, we can change the Church.

However, what do we keep seeing in all the prophetic circles? There is some kind of crisis in the world, whether political or economic, and all the prophetic wannabes jump up on their pedestals and keep babbling about what they think and feel. Taking the news headline incident as a "sign from God" they dive headlong into a monologue about its "deeper meaning."

Who cares? How does that help those that are battling? How does it set the captives free?

You can stand there and preach your sermon to the captives about how God wants them to be free. Well, until you take your key and unlock those chains, they are not free. All your ranting gets is a moment of fame on Facebook. What about doing something that lasts for longer than a minute?

You know, it is great to have an encouraging message, "God loves you. He wants to set you free of your circumstance." It encourages the heart but it doesn't make the circumstances change.

STOP TALKING AND START DOING

The only thing that brings change to those circumstances, is when a prophet stands up with that prophetic key and unlocks the door of blessing, locks the door of curses, and releases God's will into that person's life. Then, who the Son has set free, is free indeed.

It is time to stop talking and to start doing. To start accomplishing what God has intended in this world and in His Church.

There is a time to stand up and give the encouraging words. But, between the two of us – let's leave it for the guys in prophetic ministry. Okay, if there is absolutely nobody else to give the word of exhortation and prophecy, stand up and give it. It is great. But, it is time to move to a higher level now.

> **KEY PRINCIPLE**
>
> It is time to stop just giving prophetic words and start speaking those decrees and taking that key of authority that God has given you.

It is time to start unlocking those doors, start setting the captives free, and release those that are bound by satan.

It is fantastic to tell somebody, "The Lord tells you that He is there with you in your circumstance, and even though you are bound, even though you are poor, and even though you are starving, the Lord wants to meet your need."

Perfect. He feels great for a few minutes. But, tomorrow he has to face the fact that there is still no food in the cupboard. How much more is it to take that key of yours, and to release the financial blessing? How much more, to lock the enemy out of their lives, to start releasing those doors of provision for them.

GET INTO THE BIG CAR

Now, you are fulfilling your mandate as a prophet! Now you are doing something that matters in the body of Christ. Can you see the difference? What is it going to be? Are you going to sit in your little car or are you going to get into that big, fat car of yours and be seen?

You know, there is something about driving one of those big American cars – if one gets in your way it is so imposing. Good! Let's be imposing! Let's stand up and speak God's word as it needs to be spoken.

You know what? It doesn't matter if they even hear that word or not because this isn't the kind of authority that exhorts and encourages. This is the kind of decree that makes things happen.

WHEN YOU FALL, GET UP AGAIN

Unlock those doors, use that authority. Come on! I dare you. I dare you to trade in your Mini Cooper! I dare you to rise up and drive something bigger and to stand in the fullness of your authority. Do it!

Yes, maybe you are going to have a couple of bumper bashings. If you haven't driven a car like this, you are going to scrape the bumper on the side of the road a few times. It happens.

Get up again and start using the authority the Lord has given you as a prophet. Start making a difference. Now, that's what being a prophet is all about.

What Are You Releasing?

Come on. Let's shake this world. Let's shake this Church. Let's stop complaining about all the status quo leaders we are sick of. Let's stop complaining about how terrible the economy is. Let's stop complaining about hard things are today. Instead of complaining, start doing something about it.

What are you decreeing? What are you speaking forth? What are you using your key for? Are you just releasing more negativity, fear and doubt? Are you just adding to the big mountain of confusion that is in the Church right now or are you part of the solution?

We will start seeing change in this world as we have never seen because it is time for the prophets to stand up and say what needs to be said. To speak forth those words that will go forth as a double-edged sword, will cut and will bring the change.

It is time to stop sitting back and start doing and fulfilling your prophetic mandate.

CHAPTER **13**

PROPHETIC AUTHORITY

Chapter 13 – Prophetic Authority

So here it is. Prophetic Office = Prophetic Authority. Only a few questions remain, some of them being:

"What exactly is prophetic authority anyway?"

"What can I do to walk in this authority?"

"What does it look like when I have it?"

> **Isaiah 22:22** *The key of the house of David I will lay on his shoulder; So he shall open, and no one shall shut; And he shall shut, and no one shall open.*

Can you see that key in the spirit? That key speaks of the authority that Jesus held. Do you remember who set the fivefold ministry in place? Remember *Prophetic Essentials*? There, I taught you that the Lord Jesus set the fivefold ministry in place. That means, that Jesus, to whom the key of David was given, is the one responsible to put you in place and so give you some of that authority!

The Origination of Authority

So who hands out this key exactly? That was rhetorical. Jesus is the one who qualifies you to walk in that authority. Do you see why He had to come to earth? When Adam and Eve were put on this earth, the Lord gave them the authority to rule and reign.

That was short-lived though because they were hardly over the honeymoon phase when the enemy crashed the party and beguiled Eve. Next thing you know, that key of authority was handed over to satan, and man lost the power in this earth.

Can you see this picture? God gives His authority to man in the earth. Man gives his authority to the devil in the earth. God needed to make a plan to get it back. Enter... Jesus!

Fulfilling the perfection of the law, Jesus went to the cross and marched into the throne room of satan and took back the keys of death and hell. So the story has changed!

God gives authority to man. Man gives authority to satan. Jesus takes authority from satan.

Here you and I stand at the end of this story. With His hand extended, Jesus now hands you the key to the house. He delegates His authority to you, once again, to make things happen in the earth.

Now were Adam and Even walking in obedience when they gave satan their authority? Of course not! Yet... it happened anyway didn't it? Everyone gets so hung up on "losing the anointing" or on "getting the anointing" that they fail to see that it is the authority that releases the anointing.

Authority is also a gift that can only be given or taken from the one who has authority over you. In other words, authority is an object of possession.

Defining Authority

Once you understand the concept of what authority is, your training will make even more sense. The Lord has been gearing you up for so much more than a single anointing. He has been training you to function in the kind of authority that will release anointing of every kind. It means flowing in gifts and ministries of many kinds.

The limitations are about to be removed as you pass the threshold of prophetic ministry on to prophetic office.

Authority is Delegated

> **Romans 13:1** *Let every person be subject to higher authorities. For there is no authority except from God: those that exist are ordained by God.*
>
> **Matthew 8:9** *For I also am a man under authority, having soldiers under me. And I say to this one, 'Go,' and he goes; and to another, 'Come,' and he comes; and to my servant, 'Do this,' and he does it."*

This authority is delegated from the Lord Jesus. He is the one that places the fivefold ministry in place. There are no short cuts. If you want that authority, you have to get it from the Lord.

The Lord took the anointing that was on Moses and put it on Joshua. The Lord told Moses to give Joshua some of his authority (Numbers 27:10). Moses delegated his authority downwards to Joshua.

Authority is always delegated downwards, from the Lord to man. Sure, the Lord will use man to distribute his authority, but the point is that authority is delegated and not something that you can just get through an impartation!

UNDERSTANDING DELEGATION

I love Matthew 8:9. Here a centurion says to Jesus that because he is a man under authority, that Jesus must be the same. As he tells a soldier to do something, he does it, so also will this sickness obey Jesus, because Jesus clearly has the authority over sickness!

Interesting that this gentile got the concept! He "got" that Jesus was walking in authority he did not see in other men. Clearly Jesus had been given authority, by God, over sickness. This man, who was a Roman leader, defines himself as one "under authority."

There was no mistaking that he knew where he got his authority. When he ordered his soldiers around, he did so because he was given license from Caesar! When he gave an order and that soldier disobeyed, he was not just disobeying the Centurion – that soldier was rebelling against Caesar!

That is the problem in church today though isn't it? We have forgotten about the power of authority. We get so hung up on the revelations and gifts, that we forget the power that manifests them. When you speak, using the authority of the Lord and the word is not followed, it is not you they are in rebellion against – it is the Lord.

In the same way, when you tell a circumstance to change and it does not – it rebels against God! When a sickness does not leave, it is rebelling against God! Don't you understand that authority is delegated?

> ### KEY PRINCIPLE
>
> When the Lord Jesus places you in prophetic office, He hands you His key to bind and loose. He gives you authority over His house and when you use that authority, it comes with the full backing of His power.

It releases the power of the Holy Spirit to move on that person or circumstance so that it can come to pass.

WHAT IF YOU MESS UP?

So what if that Centurion gave a command that would send a soldier to his death? What if that command was unjust? That soldier dies and the Centurion realizes he made a mistake. Does his change of heart bring that man back to life? That is the price of authority. When you use it, things happen. So you better make sure, that what you are making happen is what God wants to happen in this earth.

Imagine authority as something that you can hold in your hand. It is a force and power that is independent of your righteousness and intent. It does not work only when you are doing things right. It also works when you are doing things wrong.

That means, if you speak a curse, it will hit that person like a bomb. (There are certainly defenses to that, as you learned in *Prophetic Warrior*). I am sure you have been on the receiving end of that kind of power, haven't you? Yeah... not a whole lot of fun!

You learned to overcome, but the array of arrows that those curses let loose on your circumstances was not exactly a walk in a park! Someone with real spiritual authority, praying unled, has power! It releases change in this earth! Certainly, be sure that those curses cannot alight – keep your heart pure. However, those curses still sting!

You will be attacked with circumstances and thoughts that overwhelm you. You will feel the warfare from a mile away. It's really not the kind of thing you want to hang out with on a Friday afternoon!

So realize, that authority is delegated and once it is... it is within your will to use it. Are you going to use it in obedience to God, or are you going to use it to destroy God's people?

You see the Lord removing ministers who have gone astray. Why? Yes, certainly they gave license to the enemy through their sin. However, if someone, with the kind of authority that can move mountains starts using that authority against the Church... God will step in. He is jealous over His bride.

I pray that you feel the sobering reality of your prophetic office. This is way beyond playing a game of "prophet, prophet" and on to wearing the weight of the Church on your shoulders.

Authority is a Ladder

Trace the authority that you walk in right now. You will see delegated authority everywhere you look, in the Church, your home, and the world!

All authority originates from God and is delegated downwards to man from there. God gave some of his authority to man within the home. From there, the husband delegates that same authority to his wife. His wife chooses to delegate it to the eldest child...

The Lord delegated different levels of authority to the apostles, prophets, teachers, pastors and evangelists!

Those leaders pass the authority down further. Ever wonder how someone who moves in signs and wonders delegates the authority to those under him? While that person remains in their ministry, they seem to walk in the same anointing. They leave the ministry... the anointing leaves. Why?

While they were under the authority of that leader, they were delegated some of it. When they left... they left with the portion of authority that they came in with.

DELEGATION IS SPECIFIC

So you are in a church and the pastor grants you authority over the house. That means you have been delegated specific authority. That delegated authority does not give you license to walk into the church down the road now and organize that church! You were given authority for your own house – not someone else's!

Now as you enter into prophetic office, the Lord is going to give you the kind of authority that can uproot a church or plant it.

He will not give you the authority to walk into it and structure it! That is the work of the apostle! Do you see how the delegation of authority is quite specific? The Lord has not given you the authority to change doctrine.

He has not given you authority to nurture the sheep (not unless you qualified for it.)

When you understand that authority is a ladder, it makes things quite clear. It means that you will always be under authority and that you will be in authority – delegating to others. The secret is to find your place on that ladder.

STANDING IN AUTHORITY

Now what if you are the leader of the ministry? Then you stand in authority, and it is for you to delegate that authority downwards.

BEING UNDER AUTHORITY

If the Lord tells you to submit to the authority of another spiritual leader, you do not have the authority to tell them how to change their church! That is why it is vital that you understand the difference between the local and the universal church!

For the local church, you will be under the authority of the pastor. In the universal church, you will be under the authority of the apostle. In the local church, the pastor will delegate some of his administrative authority to you.

God will delegate spiritual authority to you – giving you the power to tear down and build up!

The same in the universal church. The apostle will give you authority to build and establish with him. The Lord will give you the spiritual authority to fulfill that purpose with power!

AUTHORITY CANNOT BE "CAUGHT"

Suddenly traveling from prophetic minister to minister to "get their anointing" sounds rather foolish doesn't it? No impartation from a prophet in office is going to make you into a prophet! Sure, you might flow in a few prophetic gifts, but you will not get the authority vested in one called to prophetic office.

Let's review Simon the sorcerer. He sees the power of God come down on the new converts. He is no fool. He recognizes that the apostles are operating in an authority that he does not have. Remember... this is someone who has been meddling in the occult for some time now. He gets the concept of being given authority by a spiritual power. So he says to Peter,

> **Acts 8:19** *"Give me this power also, that anyone on whom I lay hands may receive the Holy Spirit"*

Foolish Simon. He thought that the anointing could be caught. He thought that if he just jumped through a few hoops, that this authority could just be handed to him. What does Peter say? Repent! Sort your heart out!

In other words, "If you want this Simon, then earn it! God is not going to give this authority to you until you do things His way." (My personal paraphrase of course.)

Peter really went into detail in Acts 8! He told Simon that his heart was not right with God. He told the man that he was loaded with bitterness and that he needed to repent and be forgiven. He dug deeper and said that Simon was full of poison and bound by the habits of his sin.

If Simon truly wanted to walk in that authority, it would mean getting his heart right with God and going through some sanctification!

> **KEY PRINCIPLE**
>
> You cannot just "grab" someone else's anointing that they qualified for.

You did not see the trials that they went through and the umpteen times they stood in the refining fire. Having gone through a bit of that yourself, perhaps the penny is starting to drop.

Want what that great man or woman has? There are two ways. Firstly, you can go through what they went through and so receive it from God directly.

Or secondly, you can come under their authority and they can delegate that authority to you, for the duration that you remain there.

So there you go… hopping around picking up "anointings" is not only foolish, but will only contaminate you, because you were never ready for the authority required to release that anointing!

You will flow in the anointing according to the portion of authority that has been given to you.

> **KEY PRINCIPLE**
>
> Authority is not caught, it is delegated and it takes authority to release the anointing.

Memorize that would you? It will save you the struggle of trying to get what God has for you. I am not done yet. There is a way that you can receive this authority from the Lord. I will be covering that in the next few points.

AUTHORITY REQUIRES QUALIFICATION

Here is where things really come into their own. Let's consider the authority that God had given to Moses. The day that Moses fell to his face before that burning bush, God began to delegate some authority to him. That authority was firmly established as Moses climbed the mountain into God's presence.

We visit Moses after the "plagues of Egypt" drama had died down and the screams of the Egyptians in the Red Sea had long been silenced.

Now the real work began – the work to lead millions into the Promised Land. Now Moses did not give this authority to just anyone. The first account we have is when he gave some authority to the elders so that they could help him judge Israel. Then we see him handing the rest of his authority to Joshua.

Along with that authority, came an increase in the anointing to get that job done. We see proof of that as Joshua tells the sun to stand still! He certainly got an upgrade – but it came at a price. It meant standing alone with Caleb against the reports of all the other spies.

It meant paying the price God required of him. Consider all your training and you will understand the purpose of it. You get that you need to lay down your preconceived ideas and walk in love. You get that you need your sharp edges smoothed off. What you have not realized though, is that the Lord is qualifying you for this authority.

That was what happened the day you were released into training. You got a key put in your hands. A key of authority. Consider it a "trial run" until you are placed in office and it becomes official.

> ***KEY PRINCIPLE***
>
> All this training is to qualify you to walk in the authority vested in one called to office.

Jesus spends a night on the mountain and returned in the morning to appoint the twelve apostles.

> *Mark 3:13 And He went up on the mountain and called to Him those He Himself wanted. And they came to Him.*
> *14 Then He appointed twelve, that they might be*

> with Him and that He might send them out to preach, 15 and to have power to heal sicknesses and to cast out demons:

Once he appointed them, he gave them power! In this moment, Jesus delegated his authority to them. They had to qualify first! He did not just hand his authority over to everyone that followed him. He gave His authority only to those that qualified and that the Father told Him.

To walk in the kind of authority that is going to bring change, you have to qualify for it. How many times did Jesus test His disciples? He told them to eat his flesh and drink his blood. He took them on a boat into a storm! They had to pay quite a price.

In fact, Peter says that they gave up house, home, and family to follow Jesus. They qualified. They went through the refining process and deemed themselves worthy to walk in that authority.

A Note on Love vs. Authority

Here is where you must separate the love of the Lord from His authority. You never need to qualify for the grace or love of the Lord. Those are a free gift. Jesus loved and called you, even when you hated Him.

His love as a father will never change toward you, no matter what you do. However, if you want His authority to tear down and build, you must qualify. I love all of my children the same, however I grant more authority to the eldest child in the home. Why? They have gained experience through life and she qualifies to take care of her younger siblings.

Just because I put one of them in charge, does not mean I do not love the others. It simply means that the one is ready for the authority and the other is not. It is the same regarding your relationship with the Lord.

In your striving for office, it is easy to get caught up in the thinking that, "If I qualify, then I will receive the recognition and love of the Lord." All of this training is never going to qualify to receive your heavenly Father's love and recognition, because you already have it.

His love is eternal. You will always be precious to Him. His authority though, is a power that He gives to those that prove themselves in the fire. They are vessels of honor that He can trust with this spiritual weapon.

Authority Requires Faith

Isn't it fascinating that Jesus even gave his authority to Judas, who would deny Him? As the disciples went out, they moved in signs and wonders. Along their travels though... something interesting happened. Check this out.

> ***Mark 9:18*** *"...So I spoke to Your disciples, that they should cast it out, but they could not."*
> *19 He answered him and said, "O faithless generation, how long shall I be with you? How long shall I bear with you? Bring him to Me."*

Hold the phone! What is going on here? Hadn't Jesus just given his disciples authority to cast out demons? So what is all this fuss about? They clearly had the authority, but still this demon did not leave. Why?

The secret lies in verse nineteen where Jesus scolds His disciples, telling them that they have no faith! When I read passages like this, I just have to crack up, because Jesus was just so real. I mean He did everything! He showed them what to do, went up the mountain, appointed them, and then even gave them power. Yet they still failed!

Jesus did not tell them that they did not have authority. Rather He said, that they did not have faith! You keep waiting for a greater portion of anointing – yet what you need is a greater portion of faith!

Want to see signs and wonders? When God places you in office, you have the authority to bring it to pass, but are you using that authority? Where is your faith? Are you stepping up, or are you being like the disciples? They saw an impossible situation and lost their faith.

Later on in that chapter, Jesus informs them that this sort of demon comes out through prayer and fasting. Why prayer and fasting? Well, what do you think increases your faith? Setting time aside to increase your capacity to believe releases the authority, you already have, to work!

So, see that authority in your hands right now. What portion has been granted to you? Are you in prophetic ministry or prophetic office? (I am speaking of the authority given directly from God for now, and not the authority delegated from man.)

So here we are. You hold that authority in your hand. God has said you are a prophet in office and you can tear down and build up. You can plant and uproot. You can heal the broken-hearted. You can bind demons. There it is… all the authority you need.

Do you believe it? Do you believe that the power of God has been vested in you? Do you believe that when you pray, demons will have to bow, because of that authority? You keep striving for more anointing, when what you need is more faith.

Once the faith is there, your authority will give the Holy Spirit all that He needs to move in the earth. So the seeking is over! You already have it! (If you have been placed in office). Now all you need is to step out in faith and begin using it!

Authority is Not a Feeling

When the apostles performed their first miracles, the Holy Spirit had not yet come. So no anointing from within! When they stepped out to perform their first miracles, they did so on the purity of faith and authority alone.

They could not wait for "the move of the spirit" to know that "now" was the time to speak forth healing. The Holy Spirit did not dwell within them yet, so they could not exactly count on "sensing the spirit" or "seeing as Christ sees" as they stepped out.

Nope, they had faith and they had authority – that's it! Now we have so much more than they did before Jesus died! Yet even without the indwelling of the Holy Spirit, some of that delegated authority brought about miracles.

They did not wait to feel the "breeze of the spirit." They only stepped out with faith in the authority vested into them. There was zero direction for that authority other than to "go out."

That changes things a bit doesn't it? I taught you in *Prophetic Anointing* that you need to pray until you feel the anointing. The anointing is proof that you are walking in authority! It is not the other way around.

So when you step out, very often you will feel absolutely nothing. The Lord will tell you to pray and you will not feel anything – especially when you move into speaking over nations and situations that flow over the boundaries of the local church.

KEY PRINCIPLE

Authority is not vested in what you feel! It is vested in what you have.

Do you have faith in the Lord? Do you have faith in the authority that He has given to you? Tell me something. If I woke up tomorrow and no longer "felt" like I was in charge of my ministry, would anything change? If I feel like a terrible leader, does it change the fact that my team would still follow my instructions?

What is Your Authority Reality?

My feelings have absolutely nothing to do with my reality. What is your authority reality? Has the Lord put you into prophetic office? Then that authority, is your reality. You can either choose to stand up, and use it, or not.

Now I am not saying you will get it right from the beginning, but I am saying that you need to start somewhere. You cannot sit around all day waiting to "feel" like you have the authority before stepping out into it!

There comes a time when you have to step out and use your authority in obedience with the command of God. God told Samuel to anoint David. Samuel obeyed and delegated God's authority to David.

Authority is Released

I have an iPad in my possession that I take everywhere with me. I have complete authority over it! It has my name on it. Here is a bit of reality though – until I switch the thing on, it is useless to me!

You can have all the authority in the world, but until you use it, it is useless. You are waiting for the anointing to come so that you know what to speak, however remember – the anointing is the proof of the authority you already have.

Of course you have authority on different levels. A believer has been given authority to trample over serpents and scorpions! You have been given authority in so many realms of your life. The thing is, it is only when you use it, that the authority has any power at all.

If you are waiting for the serpent to "act like it has been trampled on" before stepping on it... you are really not getting the point. Signs followed those that believed. There comes a time when you must act! You have to get your boat in the water, so that you can begin seeing things happen.

All the authority in the world can be vested in you, but until you open your mouth or take an action in obedience, nothing is going to change in your circumstances. This follows on beautifully from what I already shared in the chapter, *Prophetic Key*. Until you open your mouth and begin speaking, your authority is useless.

Until you change your revelation from a vision to a decree, it is dead in the water. Until you turn your dream into a proclamation, it is just a good idea.

Until you bind the devil, he will still run amuck. Until you release the blessing, it will remain in the enemy's hands.

On the other hand, you can "decree and declare" anything you please, but until you can do so with authority, nothing will happen!

So let's get some balance going here. Firstly, qualify for prophetic office! Once you qualify, the Lord will appoint you to that office through the agency of man. (We already mentioned this in the first few chapters.)

The moment you are appointed, you receive that authority. It is then in your hands to begin declaring God's word and bring His plan into existence.

If you are in prophetic office and God has given you an instruction – are you fulfilling that instruction? Has He told you to call circumstances into line? Has He told you to change the course of a nation? Are you speaking that out every day?

PROPHETIC OFFICE APPOINTMENT

What happens if someone placed you in prophetic office, but you feel no change? Everything is the same. Authority has not increased. Anointing has not increased. Then either they placed you prematurely and you were not ready yet, or they did not have the authority to place you.

It is very common for me to see someone who is nearing readiness to prophetic office, but that does not mean they are qualified yet.

Also, I realize that the Lord will often put someone under a mentor to receive that authority. For example,

Samuel appointed David. He did not send one of his servants to do it!

On the other hand, later in Scripture, we see how Elisha calls aside one of the sons of the prophets and tells him to take oil and go to anoint Jehu as king (2 Kings 9). Elisha delegated some of his authority to that prophet to anoint Jehu - an authority that only Elisha had to give!

So if the Lord has put you under a mentor to go through your prophetic training, that mentor has been given the authority, by God, to place you in office. If you go out of that and are placed by someone else, they do not have the authority to pass on to you! Make sure that you are really being led of the Lord if you feel to do this.

Placement to prophetic office is done through the agency of the Holy Spirit and He has an order. If He had a mentor or leader release you into training, then He has put you in their care and given them the authority to place you. Do not run around just trying to find anyone!

If you have been trained by the Lord directly, then it is quite possible that He will send you a prophet just like Samuel was sent to Saul and David.

From my personal experience though, I have seen that if I release someone into training, the Lord will have me also place them in office, even if they got their training somewhere else in between! Often it is because the Lord wanted them to receive something specific from me. Sometimes it is just to provide covering and direction.

I do not want you to draw a hard line on this. Please do not make this into a doctrine. I am just trying to help you sort through some of the pitfalls you might fall into along this journey.

Summary

The prophetic key – it is granted at the end of preparation and perfected through the training process. It is through training that you learn to walk in this authority. You learn the pitfalls and you come face-to-face with every hindrance to this authority.

Hence, the stripping and call to the cross. Once you qualify though, the Lord Jesus will delegate His authority to you and place you in office. From here, you hold the kind of authority that has the power to impact the Church.

You will hold the authority to close churches down and birth new ones. You will have the authority to sever and restore relationships. You will have the authority to heal a broken heart and bind every demon in hell.

You will have authority to put people into place in their church. You will release spiritual gifts and ministry offices. In fact, everything you learned about your prophetic purpose, you will now have the power to accomplish it.

It is one thing to talk about office and another to walk in it. As you reach this threshold though, take a long, hard look at the responsibility you will carry. Will you use this authority to bring God's promises to pass or to nurture the chip on your shoulder and vindicate yourself?

Now is a good time to visit prophetic rejection, because if there was ever something that might tempt you to use that authority on your own behalf, it is while in the throes of hurtful rejection. Watch out prophet... remember that final test I spoke to you about? It is coming...

> **KEY PRINCIPLE**
>
> Had I not known His death, I would never have known what it really means to live.

CHAPTER 14

PROPHETIC REJECTION

Chapter 14 – Prophetic Rejection

Rejection. The middle name of the prophet. What does it mean exactly? Well according to the dictionary, it is defined as:

Rejection. Dictionary Definition:

> *The dismissing or refusing of a proposal, idea, etc.*
>
> *The spurning of a person's affections.*

However, for a prophet, rejection is defined as:

Rejection. Prophet's Definition:

> *Every opposition and offense that is levied against me.*

This ranges from people rejecting your prophetic word, to someone disagreeing with the way you raise your kids. In fact, everything that makes you feel bad or insecure about yourself is lumped as "rejection" as far as the prophet is concerned.

They wear it like a badge, not realizing that these continual oppositions are the weights of the deliberate weight training of the Lord, who is trying to buff them up!

THE UGLY DUCKLING

I love the story of the *Ugly Duckling* because it so depicts you and me – the prophet. You start of as this ugly little duckling, and wow, do you face rejection. You open your mouth when you shouldn't. You say things you really shouldn't.

You don't really need to try. You just have this "gift from God" to say the wrong thing at the wrong time in the wrong place, to the wrong person. It's an ability that every prophet is born with.

If there is a way to mess something up, we are surely going to do it. If there is a way to say something wrong, we are surely going to say it. If there is a way to ruffle a feather, we are… you got it… surely going to do it. Well, that's just what a prophet is.

But you know, we don't have to stay that way. You are destined to become that beautiful swan that is admired and respected. But, there is this little phase that we call prophetic rejection still sticking to you, like gum under your shoe.

As you make the transition to prophetic office, you are still, in many ways that ugly, little duckling. When you open your mouth to try and sing a song it comes out all wrong, and everybody thinks, "What are you doing?"

The Outcast

At the core of the junk you have dealt with in training, your intentions are pure. You really think, "You know what? I am going to go help that person. I know what the pastor needs to hear. And, I know that when I tell him, he is going to be so overjoyed that I have heard from God that he is going to receive everything I say."

You get in there, you open your mouth and share your great pearls of wisdom. What happens? Well, you find out that your pearls of wisdom weren't really asked for, needed, nor wanted.

Instead of getting the recognition you wanted, he says to you what the pretty ducks said to the *Ugly Duckling*, "What are you talking about? We don't want to play with you. You are strange. You say things that are weird. You dress kind of funny too. You are just so fluffy and dramatic. People aren't comfortable around you. They don't understand you."

So, you end up as the outcast. So what is the purpose of this whole thing? Is it just God trying to be mean? Well, part of it is because we are set apart, but this is also part of your training.

The Power of Rejection

This process of rejection shapes you, and there is a very good reason for it.

> **KEY PRINCIPLE**
>
> You see, it is not the rejection that is important, but how you respond to that rejection.

You know there are so many people – I have shared this before – who think that they are a prophet just because they are rejected in life. No! Just because it is part and parcel of the calling doesn't mean you are a prophet.

But, it is certainly part of your training. How you respond to that rejection and how you handle it, is what is going to make you into something great or into something… well… not so great. Depending on how well you respond, is going to depend on how long it takes you to grow into that beautiful swan.

WHERE ARE YOU?

So let's have a look at today. Who stabbed you in the back this week? Who turned their back on you? Let you down? Upset you? Didn't receive what you had to say? So prophet, who used or abused you this week?

Am I getting your feathers ruffled yet? Are the knots inside your stomach starting to tighten? Are beads of sweat forming on your temples? Are you gritting your teeth?

Okay – right there... you are not responding very well to rejection. Once you recognize the power of rejection, the sooner you will run and jump through this final stage on your way to office.

I already shared how you will face a final test before office. Rejection has followed you throughout your life and now you stand at the dividing line between training and office.

Now is the time to transform this rejection into something that will thrust you forward, instead of always causing you to fall backwards again. Sometimes, it does feel like you are scaling a mountain and just when you feel like you are starting to make progress, you lose your footing, and fall backwards again!

Incorrect Ways to Respond to Rejection

So let's see what keeps causing you to lose your footing, shall we? Once you have a "grip" on this rejection, you can then start to use it to propel you forward!

Bitterness

> ***Ephesians 4:31*** *Let all bitterness, wrath, anger, clamor, and evil speaking be put away from you, with all malice*

The incorrect way to respond is by performing the "gritting of the teeth" thing. That's just anger turning into bitterness. That's bad. Bitterness is not a good way to respond. It is going to cause you to go in circles, and you are never going to rise up.

You are always going to face rejection. I have this reality check to share with you. The whole world is not out to get you, even though it really feels like it. But, it could very well be that *you* have something to do with why you keep facing this rejection.

If your "go to" is to get bitter and angry at the whole world, you are putting a big sign on your forehead that says, "Kick me. I am a bitter, horrible person. Please, feel free to reject me further."

IT'S CALLED A LAW OF JUDGMENT

> **KEY PRINCIPLE**
>
> Bitterness not only destroys your relationship with the Lord, but by judging others with your bitterness, you invite more rejection.

Get your hands on the message *At Liberty to Love* to help with overcoming this struggle in your life.

This is the crazy thing. You think, "Well, I have a right to be angry. They shouldn't have said that thing and bossed me around." Look, I'm not saying it is fair. I am not saying that what they did to you was right. I am judging your response to how they treated you.

By getting bitter at every offense in life, you are making the situation worse. You are destroying your relationship with God and you are just proving their case. You are proving the things that they are saying about you. There is a higher way.

Justification

> **Luke 16:15** *And He said to them, "You are those who justify yourselves before men, but God knows your hearts. For what is highly esteemed among men is an abomination in the sight of God.*

Then, of course, you got the good old justification of sin. When training any leader, this will probably get under my skin the most. You try and point out something that needs to be dealt with.

You see clearly that the Lord is dealing with a certain area in this person's life. Instead of them realizing that they said or did something to fail, they say, "You know, I was really busy this week. I didn't feel very well. I am sorry that I spewed out in bitterness. But really, I have got a headache… that is what it is.

It's because of what my husband did to me that I am forced to act this way. I didn't really mean to react badly, but the situation forced me into it."

Don't justify yourself! When the rejection comes the best thing to do is… shut up!

You know, if there was one man who could justify Himself, it was Jesus. He was sinless – yet the Scripture says that He did not offer a single word in His own defense against His accusers!

Why? Because He knew better. He could have called on a legion of angels to assist Him, but He did not do it. He knew that God the Father, would vindicate Him. You don't need to vindicate yourself.

There is no better experience than when you have messed up really badly and your boss defends you.

Well, stop trying to justify yourself, and let the Lord vindicate you. While you are so busy trying to justify yourself, you are not giving God the opportunity, and you are just looking more of a fool. Everybody thinks, "Yeah, yeah, there she goes again. She just never admits that she has made a mistake. She thinks she is perfect."

Look, whether they are right or wrong of their judgment of you, it really doesn't matter. Don't justify yourself. Let your higher authority justify and vindicate you.

SELF-PITY

> *Job 19:21 "Have pity on me, have pity on me, O you my friends, for the hand of God has struck me!*
> *22 Why do you persecute me as God does, and are not satisfied with my flesh?*

Seriously though... could Job have sounded any more pitiful? I can see a crescendo of wailing and tantrums following after that little monologue! I think there is a good portion of Job in every prophet!

Wallowing in self-pity is as bad as justifying yourself. All you are doing is getting bitter, and not only that - you are encouraging others join you in being bitter. "Shame, you were abused ... you poor thing! You are just like me – a victim to these terrible leaders."

Your self-pity causes you to overlook sin. You overlook the responsibility of each person. You fail to expose sin in their hearts because you are blinded by your own rejection.

So you have a blind spot for others. Let me tell you, if you are planning on being a mentor, you better sort this out now. Don't think of yourself as a victim. Let's scrap the victim mentality right now.

Let's realize that prophetic rejection has its place in your training. You need to respond correctly and you need to be transformed. It is not an opportunity for you to sit and lick your wounds and getting a whole "Shame, poor me, ... the whole world is against me and I am such a failure..." thing going.

By now you should have heard this quite a few times – grow up! In this phase of your journey, you should be way beyond this. You are a prophetic leader in the body of Christ. Let's rise up, and let's grow up now.

By all means, there is time for compassion, and the Lord Jesus will always have compassion. I know it is not easy. But, sitting there and wallowing over how everybody always rejects you, and never "understands" is just nonsense.

It doesn't help you at all. It doesn't help you rise up. It doesn't give you the anointing. In fact, it does quite the opposite. So... move on! Put self-pity on the cross. There is an open road before you. It's time to run.

INSECURITY INDUCED ARROGANCE

> *1 Corinthians 13:4 Love suffers long and is kind; love does not envy; love does not parade itself, is not puffed up*

The most arrogant people in the world are also the most insecure. Please prophet, don't counteract insecurity with arrogance.

It's easy to spot. You make a comment, write an article, or post something on Facebook - something fun and innocent. Then out of nowhere, someone will "come at you," spewing and attacking you.

No doubt about it...you sure hit a sore spot there!

They come at you and say, "How can you say that? How can you call yourself an apostle or a prophet?"

Now what not to do, is to respond to their arrogance with some well worded insecure arrogance of your own!

Because if you are insecure, you are going to say, "I am a prophet of God. How dare you speak to me like that?"

Listen, pick your battles! If you know who you are and who God has called you to be, you don't need to respond in arrogance. Someone that is secure in their leadership is confident to step down and not get recognition. Their recognition is not vested in their position, but in who they know they are!

The problem is that when you are insecure and somebody comes at you, you immediately respond with arrogance, trying to put them down, and pointing out their weaknesses to make yourself feel better.

You don't need to do that if you are secure in who you are. It is a wrong way to respond to rejection.

So, take a look again at all the rejection you are facing. What are you going to do about it?

Are you going to get bitter about it?

Are you going to sit and wallow in it?

Are you going to justify your way out of it?

Are you going to take the spotlight off your weakness and respond in arrogance?

Well, if I have done my job correctly, the answer should be, "None of the Above!"

Now that we looked at the ugly, nasty ways to respond. What are the good ways? Turn the page to find out!

CHAPTER 15

MAKING REJECTION WORK FOR YOU

Chapter 15 – Making Rejection Work for You

For most of your training, you have endured offense and rejection to the extreme - even taking you to your breaking point. Sometimes you responded well, other times you did not.

> ***Key Principle***
>
> Trust me when I say: Whether you responded correctly or not to rejection, each reaction has shaped you into the person you are today.

I hear prophets say to me often, "Why do I keep failing?"

"When am I going to get this right?"

"When am I going to stop going around this mountain?"

"Why do I keep tripping up… why… why… why?"

The answer is simple, because you continue to make the same mistake in the heat of the moment. When the fire comes through rejection and opposition, instead of responding correctly, you react in the flesh.

By now, you should see the rejection coming from a mile away. How about you study the points below and the next time the fire burns, make the correct decision for a change? You cannot go back and change the past, but you can surely start taking positive steps towards your future now.

CHANGE YOUR VIEWPOINT

Firstly, learn to see things from another's perspective. That is probably the most powerful of all.

I often get someone writing in, feeling that they need to warn me of my doctrine that is "most certainly going to send me to hell!"

Boy, can they be vicious! From hate mail about the fact that I celebrate Christmas (loud and proud baby!) to the fact that I am a woman in a leadership office. I kid you not… I even got a written hate mail from someone who photoshopped a traditional picture of Jesus… giving me the middle finger! (I know right?!)

But you know, you need to stop and look from their viewpoint. This is something that they really believe. They really think that they are doing you a favor by saying what they are saying.

As misguided and heretical as they are, they think that they are doing God's work. They think they are saving me from a pagan festival that will ruin my ministry and send me to hell. A tad dramatic and rather misplaced, but hey… they really think that they are called to get that word out.

Consider Apostle Paul. He was persecuting the Christians and kicking them out of their homes, thinking that He was doing God's work.

Misguided? Yes. But zealous? Most definitely.

So stop and look at the person's perspective. You know, for all you know, you remind that person of their mother, brother, sister… somebody that did them wrong.

You may have said something innocent. You may just have said "hello there" and the next thing you know, you triggered them to a pastor that they had, that put them down and insulted them.

Very often you will trigger others, especially when you begin to rise into leadership. Become a spiritual parent and there will be no end to the amount of times you will trigger people to their past relationships. You shall indeed be the wall that they splatter all their garbage against.

Perhaps they are going through a time right now where they feel very insecure, and you came across as harsh. Now, they are responding with arrogance and pride.

When you start seeing it from the other person's perspective, it makes sense. Perhaps they are pushing you away because they are hurt themselves right now and don't know how to handle it.

Changing perspective really changes you. It calms the situation down and instead of making that rejection an offense that leads to sin, it becomes an opportunity to walk in love.

STAND IN THE LORD'S SECURITY

The only way you can counteract rejection like that, is by not reacting in sin or bitterness, but by standing firm and allowing the Lord to vindicate you.

Those people fear the unknown and what they do not know. When you come with a message that they don't understand, making them feel uncomfortable, they are going to react.

Don't take them too seriously. Let the Lord reveal, and let the Holy Spirit bring conviction. You know what, maybe you are just coming across a bit pushy.

No! A prophet being pushy? Never!

Come now, you and I both know that you can get a little... passionate... sometimes. Other people don't see it as "passionate." They see it as pushy and you being a big mouth... but, what do they know, right?

God will use you for what He can do in you, regardless of your grey dirty feathers, funny looking beak and the way you squawk. God is going to take that and make it into something beautiful.

Here is the reality. People aren't just rejecting you because you are a prophet and have the anointing.

Imagine this if you will - you really do have flaws, and you are ugly. You really are a gray, ugly duckling and you talk funny. You come across wrong.

I have already explained some of this before. It is because we see things in black and white that invites so much rejection. However, you don't have to stay that way. As I promised, through this book, you are going to learn to approach people differently.

Learn to React Differently

The goal is to become a swan. The only way you are going to become that swan is by learning to react differently. When you start reacting differently to rejection, you are going to change as a person. When you change as a person, the rejection is going to stop.

Do I still face rejection now? Sometimes. I think that as any minister, you are always going to get people that don't agree with you. There will always be those that think you are weird and crazy, that women shouldn't preach and the gifts of the Spirit are not for today.

So, I think that everyone who rises into leadership receives rejection at one point or the other. However, this level of prophetic rejection that I have outlined for you in the last two chapters really does diminish considerably as you mature.

When I stand to speak now, I stand to speak with authority. I know who I am, and I don't fly off the handle every five minutes. I wait to get God's word before I talk.

I've learned to master the pendulum swinging that we discussed in *Prophetic Essentials*.

Because of that, rejection has become a tool and is no longer a hindrance. It causes me to become strong, and as a result, I do not experience it as I once used to. Turns out, a lot of the "rejection" I faced in the past was not all about the call on my life.

Turns out... I had a few things to learn about how to reach people!

You Have to Change

This is a chapter of reality checks!

> **Key Principle**
>
> The whole world is not going to change - you have to change.

You are the one that is going to be transformed.

The first step: Realize that *you* are the one being called to change.

The second step: Let go of your bitterness, your pride and your justification. It is not about whether you are right or wrong.

The third step: Allow the Holy Spirit to bring the change.

Work on your approach a little. Sometimes, you are a bit intense. Ok let's reword this - sometimes you are "a lot" intense!

Prophets are naturally intense, but it doesn't have to stay that way!

You can stand in the authority and the anointing of the Lord and you can still be something beautiful.

Making Rejection Work for You

Let's make this practical. You just got hit with rejection. What do you do? Follow these steps and start using it to your advantage!

Step 1: Rejoice

Appreciate the gift that rejection offers you. My mother left when I was fourteen… and I thank the Lord for that rejection! Had it not come, I would not have had my stepmom who I adored. I would not be in the place that I am right now, because that event triggered a domino effect that saved our lives.

When you can look at this rejection and see how much good fruit it has brought in your life, you will never regret it. It has brought up bad character traits. It has exposed things you needed to let go of – people you needed to let go of!

"I want to thank you Lord for that rejection." Does it sound so crazy to praise the Lord for your rejection? Not in a boastful way, but, when you praise the Lord, you give Him control of that rejection so that all things can work together for good.

Don't Give the Enemy any Credit

Don't misunderstand me, I am not saying that God is causing your rejection. I am not saying that He is purposefully beating you up. No, the enemy is doing a good job with that.

But you know what? I have quite had enough of the enemy taking all the credit for everything. I have had enough of him beating you up. So, why give him any more glory than he deserves?

"You know what, devil? You want to pick on me? You want to reject me? You want to give me a tough time? I am going to praise the Lord anyway. I am going to be like the prophet who said, 'I am going to praise him in the lack and I am going to praise him if the barn is full or not.'"

Ding! This changes your focus immediately. Suddenly God's in control. Instead of this rejection getting me down, this rejection is propelling me forward.

Step 2: Let It Go!

You know what I am talking about. You keep getting angry and frustrated. "They shouldn't have said what they said, and they shouldn't have done what they did."

You are right, they shouldn't have done it. The question remains though… what are you going to do about it?

Stand on top of a hill somewhere and shout to the world about how unfair it is?

So you are mad about rejections of the past. What are you going to do about it? Call up your mother and father and say, "You were mean to me?"

Grow up! It happened so many years ago. The problem lies with you and not with them.

Do you think that by holding on to all your anger, bitterness, and petty grievances that the hurt will go away? No, it is going to grow like a festering sore and it is going to stand in the way of you reaching prophetic office.

Time to Grow Up

So, step two, please kindly "Die Already" and let it go!

God has called you to be a leader in the body of Christ. Yet here you are, sitting and wallowing about what somebody did to you twenty years ago.

Let it go! Let's move on now! When you make that choice, the Holy Spirit gives you the power to let it go.

I cannot begin to tell you how many grown men I have seen whimper and whine about something somebody did to them as boys or young men. "That's why I cannot rise up in ministry. My spiritual father really hurt me and he took advantage of me…" Grow up!

This is your calling, this is your life, and this is your responsibility! God has called you, and it is for you to respond to that call! You can't say, "Sorry Lord, I can't take up the call because of what my husband did to me."

Adam and Eve tried that in the Garden of Eden and it didn't work out so well for them. And still you want to blame everybody else? You know what? It is just not worth the headache.

GIVE YOURSELF A VACATION FROM STRESS

It is amazing to me how much energy people will spend to hold on to that anger and bitterness, when it takes so little strength to just let it go and say, "Yeah, it wasn't fair, yeah, it was tough. You know what? I cannot go back and change history. I can't change the circumstance. Lord, I want to move on now!"

The problem is, because you are not letting it go, you are living in the past. You continue to remain in that memory. You are stuck in that time zone. As you continue going around in circles, dwelling on that memory, you will never make it into office.

You are stuck in a ditch digging yourself deeper and deeper. It takes so much effort to keep digging deeper, while all along there is a ladder standing right next to you. The Lord is saying, "A few steps, and you are out of there!"

When you start climbing the ladder and let it go - the clouds are going to open. Afterwards you are going to kick yourself, and say, "What took me so long?"

So, the first thing you do is say, "Lord, thank you for that pressure. Thank you for that circumstance" and then… "Okay, I let it go!"

STEP 3: DO NOT DEFEND YOURSELF

This is a tough one. So the pastor stood up behind the pulpit and spouted a bunch of lies that you know were a reference to you. You want to get hold of everybody you know in the church and set things right.

The power is not yours. Maybe God didn't want you in that church anymore. Maybe, you were dragging your feet and holding on there, and He was saying, "I want you out. I want you somewhere else."

But no… you were comfortable. So the Lord said, "Alright, I am going to shake you." And He took that pastor and He shook you. Instead of seeing it as a sign from the Lord, you end up getting bitter at the pastor. You are going 'round in circles, instead of going on to what God has for you.

Foolish! You are never going to rise up into office that way. Let it go and do not defend yourself. In fact, you are the one that has failed here because you didn't listen to the Lord in the first place. God had to take such extreme measures to get your attention.

Who cares what people think? You don't have to defend or justify yourself.

Vulnerability – a Prophetic Cuss Word

Here is the tough thing though – you really did mess up. Maybe not as badly and blown out of proportion as it was communicated, but perhaps you did say or do something wrong.

Now is not the time to put on boxing gloves. Now is the time to face the music. Do like Jesus did. He didn't come with a sword or a shield. In fact, when Peter came and cut off the ear of the servant of the high priest, Jesus healed the man.

He said to Peter, "Put away the sword. Now is not the time for swords and fighting."

Be vulnerable. When you allow yourself to be vulnerable, you are doing something very powerful – you are giving the Holy Spirit license. He has never lost a war before and He is not about to lose this one either.

Step 4: Humble Yourself

Finally, have a bit of humility. Maybe you did mess up. Maybe, you might just have failed. You know how many so-called prophets we get coming to our school saying that *everybody* has treated them badly their whole life. They state that they never did anything wrong, and all the pastors are against them.

I know, not many pastors understand what a prophet goes through, but you know, not the whole world is wrong. Could it be, just maybe, that you contributed to some of the rejection and some of the things that you are going through?

Could it be that you have a really big mouth? That you say things that you shouldn't and that you step into things that you shouldn't? That you have just a tad bit of arrogance? Could it be that you just think that you are a little bit better than everyone else?

Look at Your Failure

You know, when you are at a point where you are prepared to look at your failure, and humble yourself, God can raise you up. When you can say, "Did I make a mistake? Am I at fault here?" God can entrust His authority to you.

Now if you haven't failed, just by having this attitude of submission, you are going to be able to see the circumstance with very clear eyes.

> **Key Principle**
> When you have humility, God can step forward and vindicate you.

The scripture says that Jesus humbled Himself and became as a servant. He humbled Himself on the cross. Now as a result, He sits now at the right hand of the Father. He has power now over everything because He was prepared to humble Himself.

Do you want promotion? Do you want other people to submit to you? Do you want prophetic authority?

Then you follow these four steps for rejection. Exercise humility and let God vindicate you.

CONCLUSION

The next time rejection rears its ugly head, cling to these following steps and make the right choices!

1. Rejoice
2. Let it go
3. Don't defend yourself
4. Humble yourself

VINDICATION IS AT HAND

> **John 5:31** *If I bear witness of Myself, My witness is not true.*
> *32There is another who bears witness of Me, and I know that the witness which He witnesses of Me is true.*

Thank the Lord for His grace. You cannot control opposition and rejection, but you can choose to walk in the spirit instead of the flesh. You can choose love for hate, and laughter for bitterness. You can choose to let go and walk away.

However, even when you have failed, have you noticed something yet? Hopefully by this stage of your calling, you are starting to realize that the grace of God covers your mistakes. Hopefully, you have realized that even when you messed up, but had the right heart, God vindicated you?

There is no end to the mistakes we make as human beings… never mind spiritually minded prophets! We say things, with good intentions, but that cut deep. You speak your mind only to leave a scar.

You want to crawl away and die. Yet in these moments, the Lord not only uses your foolish words, but vindicates you. If He can vindicate you when you fail, why can He not do it when you are doing His work with all of your heart?

I want you to remember something. You have been set apart. You have committed yourself entirely to the Lord. Your life is completely in His hands. There is not a single day that you are not thoughtful of Him and that call on your life.

Now if you could see favor in your past when you were still a sinner, how much more now that your life is in His hands? Yes, much more is required of you, but it comes with some pretty neat perks! One of them being you have someone who is at your back.

He is there to cover and vindicate you.

So if you do stand up and give a prophetic word that you know is from God and that you know you have spoken in the anointing, and they reject it - they reject God.

I remember sharing a word with somebody. We were ministering to the leadership team of a church that we were invited to preach at. One of the ladies in the team asked for prayer. She was having some blockages in her spiritual life.

I didn't know her. It was the first time I met her. So I laid hands and I said, "I see a gentlemen and I sense he is somebody from your past, perhaps an old boyfriend. There is something there. You need to break that link and you need to let go."

Do you know, what she said? "No, I have already dealt with that. That's not the problem!"

I thought, "Lady, I don't know you. I have never met you in my life. God gave me this revelation." I mean, I am not walking around getting history on people's past boyfriends!

Unfortunately, she didn't want to hear it. "No, I have dealt with this. That's not the problem. It must be something else."

I looked at her and thought, "Are you listening to yourself?" It wasn't my word she was rejecting - it was God's word. God was trying to tell her where the problem really was, but she did not want to listen to it.

Now, I could not force it down her throat. She didn't receive the word. God doesn't force His will and I am not going to do it either. It is not my word. Am I going to walk away, licking my wounds because "she didn't like what I said"? Am I going to feel insulted because I got a wrong revelation? No, the revelation was spot on.

It was for her to receive or reject it. When this happens to you, don't push them. Let God vindicate you. It is God they are rejecting, not you. Don't get all personally offended over it.

It's about time that you remember who you are in the Lord. It's time that you learn to stand in your authority as a prophet.

At this stage of your prophetic journey, you have grown up a little bit. You are not that little child running around getting hurt and upset every five minutes… right?

It's time to use rejection for the purpose it was sent. Allow it to strengthen you. Allow it to give you perspective and allow it to point out the things you need to work on in your character.

It will not be long that the ugly duckling will begin to find his new feathers breaking through. Do you know what the miraculous part of all this is? After standing in your authority and being confident in your position in Christ, you will look up to see a majestic swan staring back at you in the mirror.

PART 03 – PRACTICAL PROPHETIC OFFICE

CHAPTER 16

BECOMING THE IMAGE OF CHRIST

PART 03 – PRACTICAL PROPHETIC OFFICE

CHAPTER 16 – BECOMING THE IMAGE OF CHRIST

We looked in the last chapters at how to prepare for prophetic office and also how to make rejection work for you. You are moving faster towards your goal than you realize. There are just a few more things you need to look at.

Up until now, you have learned to use your prophetic key. You have had your "trial run" and started to see some results to your prayers. In this chapter, I am going to teach you how to take everything you have learned and to increase the portion!

FROM STONES TO BOULDERS

Increase the authority. Increase the anointing and increase the impact you will have on God's people. I have labeled this section "From Stones to Boulders" because you are where Peter was when Jesus told him what I am about to share with you. Jesus had tested all His disciples and asked them who people said He was and who they thought He was. Peter did not hesitate, and said, "You are the Christ, the Son of the living God!"

In that moment, Jesus looked at Peter and said…

> **Matthew 16:18** *And I also say to you that you are Peter, and on this rock I will build My church, and the gates of Hades shall not prevail against it.*

Just like Peter, you also stand before the Lord today with a profound conviction. It is not about you. It is not about your office or power. You stand where you do today, because of Jesus, the Son of the living God! You see your limitations. Looking at the reality, you are a pebble in the hand of God.

After so much stripping, you think, "How could the Lord use me? With all this flesh and failure? With my weakness and limitation?" Yet I am here to tell you, that the little stone that you are today, is called to be a boulder tomorrow.

The stripping has brought you down to being a stone, but God does not intend to keep you there. He is about to raise you up. Prepare for office, because resurrection is coming.

> **2 Corinthians 3:18** *But we all, with unveiled face, beholding as in a mirror the glory of the Lord, are being transformed into the same image from glory to glory, just as by the Spirit of the Lord.*

So the first baby step you will take in walking in the power of the Lord, is to gaze at Jesus. It will be looking at His image in that mirror, so that the Holy Spirit can come and change you and conform you into that image.

I looked up the word "change" in the Greek, and it gave me a lovely word. It said:

> *to metamorphose, to transfigure, to change entirely from one being to another.*

Consider a caterpillar, an ugly, green, slimy little caterpillar which is not very appealing. In fact, you do not even notice it on the tree. It blends in with the rest of the trees and you do not easily see it. Unless you go looking for it, you are not going to find it.

But yet, wait for that ugly little caterpillar to wind itself up in a cocoon. Give it some time – and what happens? You get the most glorious butterfly, that when it flies across the fields, catches your eye before any other creature. It catches your eye as it flits past you. Suddenly, it is not a hidden little caterpillar that you have to seek to find, but its glory, as small as it is, is evident for everybody to see.

When you see a butterfly you stop and you gaze at its beauty. You cannot help but stop and wonder at the beautiful colors as it flutters its wings in the sunlight. It glistens and it is glorious. But it did not start out glorious. It started out as a worm.

So, are you getting the picture? Do you want to be a glorious butterfly for Jesus that brings light and sparkles in that glory? You have to be a worm first. I know that is not what you want to hear, but you have to be a worm first before you can grow some beautiful wings and delightful nature.

From Glory to Glory

There are so many different symbols used for the anointing in the Word. The anointing is illustrated as light, fire, and a cloud, but what particularly stood out to me was the oil and wine. Now how are oil and wine obtained? In the Old Testament era, they took the olives and they crushed them - they pulverized them and beat them to make the oil to burn in the lamps.

Grapes were pressed in winepresses to extract the juice to make wine.

So as we look at this chapter, I want you to know that this is the route you are going to take for the oil and the wine to pour out from you also. This chapter is about brokenness, to be conformed to the image of Jesus Christ by the Holy Spirit.

> **Key Principle**
>
> There is only one way that you are able to be formed to the image of Christ, and that is to become Christ.

You might say to me, "How do I become Christ? I am so terribly human. I have so many failures. How do you step from being so human to becoming so like Christ, to reign in glory? How do you do that?"

Conformed to His Likeness

Do you want the glory? You have to gaze at Jesus. The Spirit will work in you to conform you to the image of Christ. But it is going to take a bit of cutting away. It is going to take a bit of shaping here, a bit of chopping there, a bit of removing here, a bit of adding over there - to conform you to the image that is Jesus Christ.

In Romans 6:3-5

> *3 Or do you not know that as many of us as were baptized into Christ Jesus were baptized into His death?*
> *4 Therefore we were buried with Him through baptism into death, that just as Christ was raised from the dead by the glory of the Father, even so we also should walk in newness of life.*
> *5 For if we have been united together in the likeness (in the image) of His death, certainly we also shall be in the likeness (in the image) of His resurrection,*

So, can you see this step? In the likeness of His death, we shall be also in the likeness of His resurrection. So the first step is the step of brokenness, to be crushed like the olive and the grape, to become the image of Christ as He was in His death.

What is the image of Christ? We will look at that as we go on. We will look at the image of Christ as He hung on the tree and died, and how we shall be conformed to His death and His suffering.

I want you to know right now, before you get any ideas about walking in the anointing, that the first mantle you will ever wear upon your shoulders, will be a mantle of death.

Before you become that butterfly, you need to die in that cocoon. That is your first stage – isolated and shut in.

> **KEY PRINCIPLE**
>
> To resurrect in power, you need to be baptized into death.

What is the first step in to becoming the image of Christ - to take upon His likeness? To take upon His suffering. This whole message is carried through in all the gospels and epistles. Each of the apostles repeated themselves again and again - do you think they were trying to get our attention?

> *"That we shall be conformed to the image of Christ in the likeness of His death ... in the likeness of His resurrection."*

RESPONSIBILITY OF PROPHETIC OFFICE

What is the image of Christ? For you to walk in the glory of God means being scourged as He was. To carry upon your back, as He carried upon His back, the wounds of rejection. As He was whipped with the cat-o-nine tails, so you will be whipped. You will carry on your back, rejection. You will carry on your back the bitterness of others. You will carry on you back, opposition and everything that will stand against you in the system, in the Church and the world. Everything that Christ had to stand against, you will stand against.

You will carry on your back the rejection from the system, the rejection of those who do not understand His grace, the rejection of those who rejected Him just as the Pharisees rejected Him.

For your effort and for the anointing of the Lord, you will carry upon your back the scars as Jesus carried them - the scars of abuse and rejection, of being looked down upon, and opposed. You will never be one to seek the glory of man, but you will seek the glory of God alone.

If you need the glory of man, stop right now. You are not going to make it, because the first thing that is going to hit you will be the whip, the cat-o-nine tails on your back - the words, the biting tongues that will come against you and that satan will use to accuse you.

He lies to you and puts you down and says, "Why are you wasting your time, you unrighteous, rotten sinner? *You* are going to walk in the anointing? *You* are going to rise up in ministry? Don't make me laugh. I've seen the way you walk. I've seen your sins and how useless you are. What makes you think God will use you?"

Have you heard those words before? I have. That is the first thing that you are going to carry. There is one consolation for the words that would strike you though, and that is that you will get to bear His cross on your back. As you carry that cross, it will shield you from those words. His cross and His cross alone is what will protect you from the biting words. It will protect you from the accusation and from the bitterness that will come against you.

FITTED FOR HIS CROWN

For your efforts and for your glory, you will get to wear a crown of thorns. When you stand up for everybody to see what a hero you are, know right now that the crown that you will wear will be the crown that Jesus wore. It was a crown of splinters and thorns that cut into His head. That will be your crown - one of humility.

Why a crown? What is it that people see first about you? What do you notice first about someone? It is their face and head. I want you to know now that you will carry the scars of the crown of Christ.

That will be the face that you show the world. It will be one of brokenness and humility. It will be one of being scorned as Jesus was scorned and mocked. You will bear the splinters in your back and your shoulders. You will always bear the marks in your body of the death and resurrection of Jesus Christ.

Never think that the anointing is given for your glory. Never think that the anointing is given so that you can look so great. Your flesh, this corruptible body, needs to come to death so that the Spirit within you can come to life - so that the Lord Jesus can shine through you. So that He can take precedence in your life.

You will always bear a crown of thorns upon your head. It will never leave you. Because, while that crown of thorns is on your head, you will know humility, and Jesus can work through you.

Washed by His Tears

The Lord gave me such a lovely vision. I was in prayer and I started feeling His heart. I fell down at His feet and I started weeping. As I wept with my head down, I felt His tears washing my head and hair.

His tears were washing me and they were cleansing me, of all my fears and of all my flesh and striving. He cleansed me from all my ambition and everything that I ever tried to do in myself.

When you wear that crown of thorns, the Lord Jesus will cleanse you of all the things that you battle with. His tears will be your consolation. His tears will cover your head to cleanse you and to bring you peace and victory. But before His tears can cleanse you, you need to be wearing the crown of thorns.

Marked With Scars

For the sake of Jesus and the sake of His power, you will carry upon your hands the scars of our Lord Jesus Christ. You will carry within your hands the piercing that He had to take upon the cross. You will always know that it was Lord Jesus' work and not your own, that it is Lord Jesus' hands that healed and not your own, that it is His work and not your work. Your hands need to be dead to this world and alive to the Holy Spirit.

As we were worshipping one evening I saw the Lord Jesus come up to me. I was seeking Him to move in His power and to be used of Him. He did the strangest thing. He stepped behind me, and as He did so He stepped into me. I could feel Him step into me. His legs were in my legs, His arms were in my arms, and His hands were in my hands.

And He said to me, "When you lay your hands on another, it will not be your hands that you will be laying upon them, it will be my hands that you will be laying upon them. Never forget that. Never forget that it will not be you, but it will always be Me."

So you need to realize that as you carry the scars in your hands, His hands will come into yours and His power will come through you. As you sacrifice your works to the Lord Jesus, and submit your will to His will, His hands will come in your hands. Then you can reach those out there that need it so desperately. It will be Jesus, Jesus, Jesus - none of you, and all of Him!

WALKING THE ROAD

To walk in the glory of the Lord, you will need to bear the scars in your feet as Jesus bore the scars on His. You need to suffer the pain of the pegs being driven through your feet as they were through His. Then you will always remember that it is His path that you walk, and not your own.

It is His will that you will walk in, and not your own, so that it will never be your ideas running off at a tangent, but your steps will always be in His steps.

The Lord showed me how He was walking, as on sea sand, and He said, "Walk in My steps." As He lifted His foot to take the next step, so I would then place my feet in the step that He just took. That is how He said I should walk. "Put your steps in my steps."

Jesus said many times, *"I do only as I see My Father do."* What do you think He meant by that? I'll tell you what He meant. When He saw the Father take a step, He took one. When He saw the Father go to the side, He went to the side. He imitated His Father step by step.

That is what we need to do with the Lord Jesus. If He turns to the right, you need to turn to the right. If He walks into the slums, are you going to walk with Him or are you going to stay in your nice, clean, neat little home - all warm and safe?

Are you prepared to walk where the Lord is walking? I want to tell you - He does not have any restriction. He does not just walk in the nice parts of town. He walks where the prostitutes are doing business. He walks in the slums where the beggars are starving.

I want to tell you, that is where the feet of Jesus walk. He walks where there is death, He walks where there is sin, He walks where there is emptiness, and He walks where there is sickness.

Are you prepared right now to make that decision to walk where Jesus walks? He walks in the midst of abuse in the vilest of sins and crimes that you have not even come to understand. Are you prepared to place yourself in that position to walk where Jesus walked? Or are you safe at home saying, "Lord, give me the anointing and Your outpouring, that I may minister to those in my church?"

Let me tell you, Jesus is not just sitting on the pews each Sunday. He is sitting and weeping in the alleys, the ghettos, and the slums where people are dying and crying out for Him. Are you still going to tell the Lord that the church He sent you to, is not good enough for you? Are you still going to run after each new move and "revival" instead of realizing that He sent you to the dead and dying church you are in, for a reason?

Everyone wants to walk the road of the megachurch, but what if the Lord has humbled you and sent you to a little "mom and pops" local church to change just one life?

Are you prepared to wear the shame and the loincloth that He wore? Will you trade in your garments of beauty for rags? That is the price you will have to pay if you want to flow in His power and His anointing - to walk where He walks - to always know that you will be walking in that blood that came from His feet.

The minute you step out of that trail of blood, you are not going to be in His will.

EYES TO SEE

But be encouraged, because when you walk in that blood, you walk in His protection. You walk in His divine will and there is nothing that you cannot do in this world with His power in your hands and His feet in your feet.

> **KEY PRINCIPLE**
>
> There is nothing you will not be able to do for the Kingdom of God. He will give you what you need, if only you are prepared to give up what you have.

He will give you that and more if you are prepared for your hands to be pierced. If you are prepared for your feet to be pierced and to walk in His will.

He will reward you with His power, because you will become Him. He will be in you, and you will be in Him. It will no longer be your ideas - it will no longer be what you want to do. It will be, "Jesus, where shall we go today?"

You might be surprised on Sunday morning when you say, "Jesus, where should we go today?" and He does not say to you, "Let's get dressed and go to church." He says to you, "Pick up a bag. We're going downtown. There are a couple of backsliders there I want you to talk to."

Would you be prepared to do that? Would you be prepared, as Jesus was prepared, to lower your human standards to walk into corruption as He did? You know He could have sat pretty with the Pharisees and looked like a real hotshot.

He was not a stupid man. He amazed them at twelve with His knowledge of the Word. Jesus could have risen up in social standing. He could have been one of the big names and the best teachers that they had ever known and they would have all looked up to Him.

But no, where did He choose to spend His time? He chose to spend His time with a bunch of fishermen who did not know any better - who were looked down on by society, and who stank of fish.

That is who Jesus spent His time with, not with the pleasant well-anointed, sweet smelling Pharisees. Because to Jesus the anointed Pharisees stank more than the fishermen that were perfumed by fish guts!

He preferred the fishermen, because He saw something in them nobody else did. Are you prepared to see something in others that nobody else sees? Are you prepared to look at the rejects that nobody wants to be with, and the lost little sheep that have been thrown out of the fold?

Are you prepared to see them as Jesus sees them? Or are you going to bear in yourself the suffering and the death of the Lord Jesus Christ, and walk on from glory to glory?

A Point of Decision

You see, the choice is yours. The Lord Jesus will never impose it on you. He is standing there as we said in Scripture, and you can see His image in the mirror. Now you can choose to look at the image, or you can choose not to. You can choose to gaze upon that image and allow the Holy Spirit to transform you into Him, or you can choose to look away and go your own way.

You see the Lord Jesus is not going anywhere, and He is not forcing you to do anything. You need to know this. He is not forcing this on you. This is your choice. If you really want that power, if it burns in you so badly that you cannot sleep at night, and when you wake up it is like you have a knot in your stomach - if you want it that badly, then turn right now and put your gaze on Jesus.

As you do that, the Holy Spirit will come, and I can tell you what He is going to do. He will put marks upon your back. He will put a crown of thorns upon your head. He will put scars on your hands and He will put scars on your feet. That is what it means to be conformed to the image of Christ.

A Heart Torn in Two

I left the most important part for last. To be conformed to the image of Jesus Christ means to have a broken and pierced heart. As Jesus hung on the cross, they came and thrust a spear into His side, and blood and water flowed. This means that He died of a broken heart.

It was not only broken - it was pierced as well. The Lord Jesus bears in Himself the suffering of a broken heart continually. You need to have the heart of the Lord Jesus within your breast, and it needs to be continually broken before Him.

The Lord Jesus gave me the most awesome revelation of this. As I was communing with Him, I saw that He was weeping. I could not understand and thought, "Why is the Lord Jesus weeping?" It really affected me so much! He showed me His heart and it was bleeding. It was running with blood, and was torn and broken.

I was so confused I said, "Lord Jesus, what is going on?"

He said, "I weep and bleed for my people. I weep and bleed for the little sheep that have been led astray. I weep and I bleed for the little sheep that have been broken and left to die - for the runts that nobody wants to have anything to do with.

I weep for the sheep that have not even been found yet, because nobody is going looking for them. I weep because I see their pain and I see their heartache, and I know that I have everything to offer them.

I do not have human hands, I do not have human feet, I do not have human lips - but you do. If you will be my human hands and my human feet and my human lips, I will give you my tears to bear, and I will give you my heart, so that you can go out and reach those for whom I weep so much."

Passion for Jesus

That, I believe, is the promotion we need to be aiming towards - which is to bear in ourselves the broken heart of the Lord Jesus. God is love. He ministers from His heart, and we also should be ministering from His heart.

We can only minister from His heart if we have that heart in us, and it will only come through brokenness. It will come by taking that grape and crushing it. That is how you are going to have the heart of Christ. To be broken before Him, to be nothing, to start out as a worm. It is not a nice place to be.

Is your training making sense? You cannot look now at those who are crushed and not feel their pain – because you have been there!

As you rise up in authority you will come to the place where you are weeping His tears - where you are feeling His blood pumping through you. Where you know throughout your whole being what He feels, what He wants, and what He is saying, so that you can act upon it.

You will not come to that place unless you surrender yourself to it. Unless you surrender yourself to His death and surrender yourself to being crushed and broken- to being nothing but a little stone - you will never know His tears and you will never know His heart until you come to that place of brokenness.

THE REWARDS

I know that the price seems so terribly high. But oh the rewards! Just the reward of knowing the Lord Jesus Christ.

To know Him and walk with Him and talk with Him, and to have Him within you and so madly in love with you. In fact, just to have that, and not even the authority and the anointing, is enough.

It is enough just to be so madly in love with Him that you cannot wait to be with Him - that when you wake up He is the first thing on your mind. When you drift off to sleep, you are speaking to Him. To just have that in your life far outweighs any treasure - far outweighs all the gold in the world. When you can get to that stage, the authority and anointing will mean nothing to you.

When to be shut away with Jesus and know His heart is what you desire and the power and the glory and the anointing mean nothing to you, you have finally come to the place of being a little stone. You finally are becoming something that the Lord can start to use.

CHAPTER 17

RESURRECTION: BECOMING A ROCK

Chapter 17 – Resurrection: Becoming a Rock

Give Him Your Heart

Allow what you have just read in the previous chapter to soak into the recesses of your heart. Allow the brokenness to release the power of God within. For it is when we are brought to the end of ourselves and crushed by His hand, that the gold that is within is revealed.

Allow the death to wash over you and bring out the greatest treasure of all – Jesus Christ.

> **Philippians 3:10** *That I may know Him and the power of His resurrection, and the fellowship of His sufferings, being conformed to His death,*

To have the glory is not only to experience the sufferings and the death, but also to be glorified with Him in resurrection.

To become a boulder, you need to start as a stone. To become as a butterfly, you need to start as a caterpillar. To know the power of His resurrection means to be conformed to His death.

Can you see it? Are you starting to get the picture? Is His Word, His voice, starting to churn in the middle of your stomach? Do you hear Him tugging at you saying, "Child, this is what I want for you… come."

Hear His voice even now saying to you, "I have so much for you. Do you want to love me? Don't you want to know me? I want to know you. I want you to know my voice, I want you to bear my heart, I want you to bear my tears for my people."

Can you hear Him speaking these words in your ear? Because I want to tell you something, you do not need to be special to know the Lord Jesus Christ. You do not need to fast for forty days and forty nights to know Him in this way.

You just need to want Him. You just need to desire to love Him.

> **KEY PRINCIPLE**
>
> All that the Lord has ever required of you since the day you were saved, is your heart.

TO SIMPLY WANT HIM

Are you prepared to give that to Him? Are you prepared to not only invite Him in to that little space, but to let Him live in it, and live through it - to be changed to what He is? That is all He wants of you. He wants you. He does not want your works. He does not want your fancy prayers. He does not even want your money. He wants you, as you are, rotten and imperfect, looking like a caterpillar.

That is all He wants, just you as you are - a pathetic little sheep straying away from the flock. A little nobody, the one with the broken leg that nobody mended.

It is no coincidence that the Lord always used sheep to symbolize His people. They were not considered very high on the scale of intelligence. Sheep were not considered something to be looked upon with awe. Have you ever seen a sheep?

It is not a bright creature. It is not something that you stand back and say, "Wow! That's a sheep!" Sheep do not inspire awe. They are stupid creatures. They stray off for nothing. All they know how to do is have babies and eat.

But yet Jesus compares us to sheep. He says, "I love you so much. You're so special. When I look at you I don't think, 'What a dumb little sheep.' I look at you and I think, 'Wow, I'm going to raise you from glory to glory.'"

That is what Jesus sees in you. You may feel like a dumb little sheep that has nothing to offer - that all it can do is stand in the corner and go "Baa." But Jesus sees more in you than that. Jesus wants to gather you in His fold and He wants to give you the most precious gift you can ever know - His heart and His tears.

THE SECRET PLACE

The Lord gave me such a beautiful experience of this. I came to Him and I was just so in awe of His presence, and I bowed down. I was in the Throne Room and everything was so glorious. The angels were singing and I was in awe. I just could not believe the majesty that I saw. I fell on my face and did not want to look up.

I looked down and I opened my eyes and saw these feet sticking out from beneath a robe. He stood up, and as He stood up I saw that His feet were pierced. As I was weeping before Him, the Lord Jesus bent down and He lifted my face up so gently. He looked into my eyes and said, "Come."

He said, "Stand up My child, come with Me."

He took me by the hand and led me out of the Throne Room, with all the glory, gold and the power. He took me to a garden. In this garden was a brook. Whenever I get into the Spirit, even now, I can hear the sound of that bubbling stream as it flowed through this garden. Next to the brook stood a huge willow tree.

I have such wonderful childhood memories of willow trees. They always brought me such comfort, and I used to play hours and hours underneath them, so I guess that is why the Lord uses that for me. He knew that was my special place that I used to go to as a child.

He then sat me down beneath this beautiful big tree, and just plopped down next to me as casual as you can be. He just sat there and looked at me and smiled. He did not expect anything from me. He did not expect me to worship Him, He did not expect me to give anything to Him. He just wanted to be with me.

At first, I did not know what to do with myself. I mean, I am with my Lord and Savior, Almighty God… and He just wants to look at me for a bit? I did not know what to do.

He sat and waited, as if He knew what I was going through. Eventually I started to talk to Him and He spoke back. Ever since then, that is the way it has always been between us.

He just wants to sit and talk with you. As you talk with Him and as He talks back, something incredible will happen. As you gaze on His face constantly, the Holy Spirit will work on you to conform you to the image you are focusing on.

Falling in Love Again

It was the beginning of a journey that keeps me going today. Like a bride full of the romance of the honeymoon, I remember my naiveté and how much that naiveté formed me into the prophet I would become.

I remember times when I was upset and would get away from everyone to go and just lie in His lap. I will never forget the one time I came to Him. It was the most special moment to me. He covered my face with kisses like you would a little child.

At that time, my eldest two daughters were still very young and there was nothing more precious to me than these two girls. They were so cute, and I would I often pick them up and give them hundreds of kisses all over their faces just because they were so adorable and meant so much to me. In the same way the Lord Jesus took my face in His hands and He kissed me all over my face like I was a little child.

He said to me, "You're so adorable, you're so cute. I love you so much."

It did something. I started getting His heart. I started feeling what it was like to be Jesus. I started feeling what it was like to weep. And that is how it needs to be. It is not something that will be forced on you. It is not something that you have to do – Step 1, Step 2, Step 3, like a regimented soldier.

No! It is getting away to a secret hiding place and being with your Jesus. It is being with the lover of your soul, your best friend, your father. He is the most precious and wonderful person you will ever know. He looks at you and He adores you. He adores you more than His life. In fact, He would die again just for you, because you are so precious to Him. He just wants to sit and look at you.

On the race towards prophetic office you forget those times and I pray that as I share, that I am triggering some memories for you also. You have become a great big warrior for the Lord. You have fought the demons of hell as you worked through *Prophetic Warrior*.

However, remember this – when your arm is tired and your sword has been put away, you are still a child that very much needs the affection of their Father.

A father that watches over you as you sleep. I was drifting off to sleep one night, and in vision I saw the Lord Jesus lying there next to me. He was just stroking my hair and looking upon me with this gaze of pride and love. Have you not done the same with your own children?

I look at mine while they sleep, and as I look at them I think, "I'm just so proud to be your mom. I'm just so proud the Lord gave you to me. You are so precious to me."

That is what Jesus feels for you. I can tell you right now, all the thorns and the nails and the piercing are worth it. It is worth it, to have Him look upon you and say,

"I love you so much. You are so special to me. You know what? You're so special to me that I want you to carry my heart. I want you to carry my tears. You're so special to me that I want you to be my hands. I trust you so much that I am going to trust you with my sheep. You know those sheep that are gems to me? I trust you and love you so much that I'm going to let you go and look after my sheep."

To me, there is no greater privilege than to have Jesus stand in my body and work through my hands.

SMALL BEGINNINGS

> *Matthew 16:18 And I say also to you, that you are Peter, and upon this rock I will build my church; and the gates of hell shall not prevail against it.*

You might be looking at yourself now and thinking, "Yeah, that's me. I'm just a little piece of rock. I am just a caterpillar."

But I want you to realize that Peter did not stay that way. If you look up the Greek for *"rock"* here, it is not just a rock, but it is a ledge of rock. It is a whole building of rock. You might start off as a tiny little stone, but sooner than you think, as you gaze upon Jesus and allow the Spirit to work through you, He will start building upon that rock.

He will start adding to it. You seek first the Kingdom of God and His righteousness, and all these things will be added to you.

You may start out as a little stone, but as you seek Jesus, and you seek His face you will be added to.

You will not be sitting around thinking, "Have I been added to today?" It will not even be in your thoughts because you will be so consumed, so in touch with the Lord Jesus that the external will not matter anymore.

You will not care anymore for your own desires. You will not care anymore for your own flesh. All that will matter will be the Lord Jesus Christ and what He wants.

How to Minister to Jesus

You will be saying, "Lord, what do you want me to do for you today? Lord Jesus, do you have a need? Would you like me to minister to you?" That is the place you need to come to.

You were created for the Lord. The Lord was not created for us. We were created to worship Him. That was why we were created - to minister to our Lord and Savior. If you can minister to Him, He will say to you, "If you want to minister to me, then minister to my people."

Remember when Jesus said, "You saw those who were hurt and you did not help them, and those that were hungry and you did not feed them. When you did not feed them and did not heal them, you did not do it to me. But those that you did clothe, and those that you did feed you did it unto me." (Matt 25:42)

That is what it means to minister to Him - to heal and to feed and to love those He sends you to.

> **KEY PRINCIPLE**
>
> Do not be discouraged if you are feeling like a little stone, because upon that stone the Lord will build a rock. And upon that rock He will build His Church.

YOUR MUSTARD SEED

The Lord Jesus said, "To what shall I compare the Kingdom of Heaven. I shall compare it to a mustard seed, that when a man plants it and it grows it becomes a huge tree that the birds nest in its branches and the animals can come beneath it." (Matt 13:31) You might be nothing but a mustard seed right now, but give Him that mustard seed.

If you have nothing within you and you say, "Father, I don't have the hope. I don't have the faith. I don't have the love. I have a little bit. I have a little bit of desire and I have a pinch of love."

Give Him your mustard seed of faith and He will grow a tree out of it. But give Him your doubts and He can do nothing with them.

Give Him a boulder and He will make it into a stone, but give Him a little stone and He will make you a ledge.

Give Him a huge mustard tree and He will cut it down, but give Him a seed and He has something to work with. He has something to raise up into glory.

Give Him the little bit that you do have. There is a flame in you. It is a small flame sometimes, but it is there, and it is burning. It has been burning since the day you were saved. Do not think that you were left out.

Now it might be the size of a mustard seed. It might be tiny and it might look insignificant next to these great heroes of faith. However give Him that tiny little burning, that tiny little desire and passion, and He will fan it into an inferno. Give Him what you have and He can work with that.

But do not look at yourself and say, "I would rather just not look at the image of my insignificance," because then you will lose out on the glory. Rather give Him what you do have. Say, "I might just be a caterpillar, but hey, if you can do something with the caterpillar, Lord, here I am."

He will say, "I have a plan. I'm going to make you into a butterfly. That's a good idea. You might look like a nothing now, but I tell you what, little caterpillar, come sit with me a while. Come and hide in your cocoon with me a while. Come into my secret place. Come into my chambers. Step into my office…"

And when you walk out of there, you will walk out of there a brilliant butterfly.

Going Through the Process

I would like to end off with something really special the Lord gave me when I was starting out in the honeymoon phase of my face-to-face relationship with Jesus. I hope it takes you back to the same place it took me, reviewing this once again. It is a prayer that came out of my spirit when He gave me the revelation of the Cross for the first time.

> *I surrender all to my Savior. He is my Savior from emptiness, despair and mostly myself.*
>
> *I gave Him my head, that I might wear His crown of thorns to remind me of my humanity. Knowing that as I wear the crown that pierces, His tears*

will pour upon me always, bringing His healing and His glory.

As they whipped my precious Savior and tore His back, may I bear in my body the pain of being scorned from behind. As I carry upon myself the scars of rejection and the scorn and bitterness of others, Lord, give me your cross to carry, that it might keep those words hidden from me. Lord. I will gladly bear upon my shoulders and back the splinters of your cross, because I know that when this corruptible flesh is on the cross, you can reign through me.

I yield unto you my hands so that they might be pierced as yours so that your hands can be in mine. I give you my feet so that the steps that I take are your steps, and the path I walk is ordained by you. May I never walk in my own will. Jesus, guide my steps that I may always walk in your blood.

And finally, Lord Jesus, more than anything, let me bear your heart, as it is pierced within me to show my brokenness. Let your life's blood never cease to pour from me, cleansing me and giving me life.

I know that as I remain crucified in Christ, His blood covers me and His light covers me. That is why I rejoice in these times of testing and trials, because had I not known the scourging I would not have known the cross.

Had I not known the crown of thorns I would not have known the tears of His mourning.

Had I not known the splinters of the cross I would never have known the power of His cleansing blood.

Had I not had my hands pierced, I would never have felt how His grace brings power to them.

Had my feet remained whole, I would never have known the joy to dance in the fields of glory, unrestrained and passionate for my Savior.

Had I not known the piercing in my side, I would never have known His power.

CHAPTER 18

INCREASING THE PROPHETIC ANOINTING

Chapter 18 – Increasing the Prophetic Anointing

When I was growing up, we stayed on an acreage and we were really blessed because we had a borehole. Well, I don't know if we were really blessed because, sometimes, because we had the borehole, the water could be a little brown. If things got dry, the water got low. So that meant we wouldn't have water in the house.

Having a borehole, is a very fascinating concept. When there was rain, the water would go into the underground stream, and then we had the windmill which would turn and pump water from that stream and onto the house.

As you went through the process of being stripped, you came to realize that you have living waters inside of you. Just like I reminded you in the last chapter – you have the fire! You already have what you need.

I have challenged you to grow. I have told you that it is possible to start as a stone and move on to becoming a boulder! Now let me take you by the hand and show you how to do that practically.

How can you take the portion of anointing that you already have and increase it? Well the secret is quite simple.

Increasing the Prophetic Anointing

Firstly, you already have it, just like you learned in the *Prophetic Anointing* book. Secondly, because you have come into an intimate relationship with Jesus, you have that water source "on tap" any time you need a top up!

PROPHETIC ANOINTING REMINDER

The main thing that I want you to see clearly is that the prophetic anointing is an internal anointing. In other words, it isn't rain that gushes down and pours down on the land, but rather it sits in underground streams and bubbles up and is fed outwards.

Now, this can be confusing when you are used to soaking in the rain. You are used to the anointing coming down, and to feeling it tangibly from "out there." You are used to standing and the Holy Spirit does all the work.

The great thing about the external anointing is that it doesn't matter what state your spirit is in, it is really up to the faith of the people. You stand there, and God moves.

The prophetic anointing is very different though. It is much gentler and it is quiet. I am hoping that I can help you identify it so that you realize that you are normal, that you are flowing in the anointing, and also how to tap into it at any time.

Anointing on Tap

You see, that's the great thing about the internal anointing. Once you are filled up, you can tap into it at any time.

The rains come when they will. When it comes to the external anointing, it comes when God wills and as you stand in faith. But, the internal anointing is always there.

You can tap into it every time you speak in tongues, every time the Lord uses you to give a prophetic word, every time you get into intercession, and suddenly you start flowing in all the gifts of revelation.

All of that is the prophetic anointing. It is not coming from "out there."

I have come to see that the Lord will often move somebody from the evangelistic ministry to the prophetic. The evangelistic is all about the external anointing. The ministry of the evangelist is towards the world, and you will see its fruit in the super duper prophetic words about the nations and what God is going to do in the world.

Prophet - Love the Church

You have a different heart though. You bear in you the aching of the Lord Jesus. You are in love with the Bride that He is in love with. You want to see her without spot and wrinkle. It is because of your intimate relationship with Jesus that you have been given the anointing to equip the Church.

It can be confusing at first though. When He shifts your ministry, you might still prophesy, but the way you operate is going to change. It is going to change to words towards the Church, to words of exhortation and encouragement.

Instead of feeling the anointing on the outside all the time, you are going to feel it on the inside. If you don't expect this shift, you are going to feel lost. You will be waiting for the big storm cloud that you think will come.

Instead, all you are going to feel is this stirring deep inside of you. It will come as a trickle from inside.

It is in Your Spirit Already

You see, God is speaking to you all of the time. It doesn't matter what time of the day. Why? Because He resides in your spirit. You can tap into that, and you don't need to wait for the thunder flashes anymore.

You don't need to wait for the big signs and wonders to hear His voice.

You don't need to wait to be able to reach out and minister. You have got everything that you need right inside your spirit. The problem is that you are just not identifying it or releasing it correctly.

HOW TO RELEASE THE ANOINTING

So the million-dollar question is… how? How do you increase the anointing that God has given to you as a prophet?

Well the way not to do it is by looking up and asking, "Lord, when is it coming? More Lord! Bring the rain."

Chill out, it is not coming from "out there." It is coming from within.

The problem is: How do you pour it out? The first thing you do is start praying in the spirit.

1. PRAYING IN THE SPIRIT

You need to start praying in tongues more and speaking in the spirit more. As you do that, that little trickle will start to become a bubble, which will become a stream, and which will become a raging waterfall.

When you realize that the anointing doesn't come from the outside, but it is already there, you have something that you can start working with.

> **KEY PRINCIPLE**
>
> You are not dependent on the mighty rushing wind. You can tap into the gentle breeze of Jesus anytime.

Even if you don't get revelation, even if you don't get a word of direction for somebody, you can still lay hands on them and release that anointing. It's actually a choice.

I want to remind you to speak in tongues more! That muddy water will be made clean. Remember how you learned to speak in tongues for an hour to "clean your spirit"? When last did you do that again? When last did you take time to speak until your mind cleared?

The truth is, the more you get into active ministry, the more you will feel everyone's conflicts around you. You try to pray or journal and your mind is harassed with all the cares around you.

You will be harassed with thoughts about your responsibilities and the conflicts that others are going through right now. If you want the anointing back, it's time to do some housecleaning! Get back to speaking in tongues for long periods of time to build up your spirit.

2. Release it by Faith

I especially learned to do it when I was preaching. I realized that there is a way that I could just step into His mantle, step into His anointing, and release it by faith.

The most exciting thing is that you have the same spirit that raised Jesus from the dead living inside of you.

Now, Apostle Paul went to the Lord and he said he sought the Lord about having his thorn in the flesh removed. But, the Lord said to him, "My grace is sufficient for you." (2 Corinthians 12:7-8)

He already had the answer. He already had the grace. He already had the power to overcome. The problem is you keep looking to the Lord to do things for you. You keep looking for this wind and for this "something" to come down upon the people, not realizing that you are the vessel.

The Wine

You are the vessel that is already filled up to the top with wine. That is what the crushing was all about. The grapes were crushed and Jesus filled you with His wine. All you need to do is pour it out in faith.

You need to be filled up. When you are filled up, the Lord can pour you out. That is the whole concept of the prophetic anointing.

3. Enlarge Your Vessel – Top Up!

To pour out, means that you have to top up. I find that if I have been doing a lot of ministry, I can get really drained, really fast. That is why the prophet's "go to" is always the presence of the Lord Jesus.

You are not any better than Jesus and He took time to fill up every night. Often you read of Him hiding away in the presence of the Father. I want to ask you today – do you want to just "maintain" your ministry, or do you want to go to a new level?

Increasing the Prophetic Anointing

Then you need to do a lot more than just replenish what has been poured out. You need an increase. Remember *Stones to Boulders*? You are back there again. Each time the Lord calls you to the cross, your vessel is increased.

> **KEY PRINCIPLE**
>
> Each time you are conformed to the image of Christ, you are shaped into a vessel that has the potential to hold more wine.

Now, you can keep "topping up" or you can increase your measure.

Increase your measure by:

1. Paying the cross a visit
2. Soaking in His presence

If you take the time to go through the "stones to boulders" process and then remain in that secret place long enough, you have that anointing on tap anytime you need it.

You don't have to wait for it. That is what is great about the internal anointing. Get into His presence, feel His presence and have a good time with Him. When I say that, I see a beautiful big vase that gets filled as you get into His presence.

As you speak in tongues it starts to fill you up, until you are at the point when you are ready to start flowing over. When that happens, you are ready to start dipping into that for ministry at any time. Whenever God needs you, you will be equipped and ready.

Feeling the Lack?

Are you finding that the prophecies have become a little less frequent? The revelation isn't flowing quite as it used to? God isn't using you as much?

You feel a lack like a beautiful golden ornament that suddenly starts to tarnish, is dull, and is not as shiny as it used to be. Time for refining and a top up!

4. Keep on Track

You know what the enemy does to distract you from doing God's work? He has you so busy running around "doing the work of the ministry" that you end up emptying yourself out on things that God did not intend for you.

You are so busy sorting out people, circumstances that you forget the essentials of, "Doing as I see my Father do." You end up running around and pouring out all this wine and water, on everything else that when somebody does come for ministry, you are so finished that you don't even have a drop left to spare.

Consider how much time Jesus spent in the presence of the Father. He was the Son of God, and He spent so much time in the presence of the Father filling up

Increasing the Prophetic Anointing

continuously. Now, if He as the Son of God, had to keep filling up and keep staying in His presence, I think you and I know where we stand!

The Apostles followed Jesus' example. Consider how much time they spent in His presence, to be able to pour out. They were smart because they caught onto the enemy's tactics really early in the game.

> *Acts 6:2;4... It is not desirable that we should leave the word of God and serve tables*
> *4...but we will give ourselves continually to prayer and to the ministry of the word.*

They realized that they spent more time "serving tables" than doing the work that God called them to. I am not saying it is not a ministry, I am saying: Do not get caught up with what is not your ministry.

If you have nothing in you, you have got nothing to give to anybody else! The Apostles (whose shadows healed the sick) dedicated their time to prayer and study of the Word. A change of focus is needed here.

> **KEY PRINCIPLE**
>
> Don't get so busy running around in works, that you forget that the power is in the anointing and that the anointing is available inside your spirit.

Chapter 18

FLOW IN THE ANOINTING ALL THE TIME

What is coming out of your mouth when you sit down to minister? Logic? What you think? Your great advice? Or, is it the anointing that is coming out when you speak? I am not just talking about ministry. I am talking about all the time because you should be flowing in the anointing all of the time.

When somebody comes to you for counsel or when you need to make a decision, how much of that time is being spent trying to figure things out with your mind, instead of flowing in the anointing?

It is so simple. Everything you touch can prosper. Everything you do can flourish. Every word you speak can be anointed. Every decision you make can be the right decision. Your ministry can go right. The Lord can open those doors.

However, it begins and it ends with the anointing. Without the anointing, what are we? We are just like the world. We are just doing the work. We are just pressing on through.

The problem is that you have exhausted yourself so much that you are very, very dry.

YOU KNOW THE MOTTO: ALWAYS BE PREPARED!

You need to be prepared in and out of season. That means getting your spirit in line. God will move on you, but just get yourself in line. Yes, God is gracious, He will even use you in spite of yourself.

But like I asked before, is the anointing drying up in your life? When you preach, are you seeing the effect of the anointing on the hearers? Are you flowing in revelation?

Is it easy or are you having to really dig the anointing out? When there is oppression around or you know that you are in the presence of someone that has a lot of demonic activity in their life, are you feeling the demons? Are you feeling oppression?

I know that sounds crazy... But, when I stop feeling oppression, then I start worrying. The gift of discerning of spirits is one of the first the Lord usually uses me in, so if I am in a place where I know there is demonic activity and I do not feel anything... either I am operating as a teacher, or my spirit is blocked!

When the gifts are becoming dull, it means that you have not taken care of your spirit.

Your Spiritual Fitness Routine

Consider how much money you spend in this modern age on face care, hair care, body care, health care and gym subscriptions to tone your body.

Look at how much money you spend on books, and even on learning, and studying. You are feeding your mind, your will, and your emotions.

Now how about your spirit? When was the last time you fed your spirit so that the anointing could flow out of you? When was the last time you conditioned your spirit and made it "fit"?

Hear His voice. Start journaling again. Start receiving from Him again. Get back into His Word. Start speaking in tongues. Then, once you have done that, pour it out and minister to others. As you receive and pour out, the Lord will increase your vessel.

THE WORKOUT INVESTMENT BRINGS INCREASE

It is like you start off as a little oil jug. You fill it up and pour it out. You fill it up and pour it out. The more you do that, the more it will grow. In the same way, so will your capacity for the anointing grow and grow.

You can progress in the anointing. You don't have to stay where you are. However, it means filling up and pouring out. It is a very simple progress.

EAT A PROPER DIET

Listen to some teachings. Pop an anointed mp3 into your player. Listen to it and charge up. Hear His voice, read the Word. Just lock yourself away for a little while and top up again.

Suddenly, the noise out there will start to quiet so that you can hear that bubbling brook from deep within. You will start to hear that still small voice.

What is awesome when you minister with that anointing is that it soaks deep into the hearts of God's people. It is water that splashes on that dry ground and brings all the seeds to life - it is a continual river.

It is not like a thunderstorm that comes and goes. The internal anointing continues to feed. It continues to minister.

CHANGING POWER

When you lay your hands on someone and you speak that anointing into their lives, it will enrich them so much that they will go away with their problem solved.

But to give it - you have got to have it to give! The Lord's warehouse is unlimited. The question is, how much of it can you hold? Well, it is about time you start finding out.

Start filling up with it. Start reveling in it. Start soaking in it so that you are so saturated with it people will just get wet every time they come near you.

You splash them with the anointing everywhere you go. All these little problems you keep facing will get washed away. If you try to deal with these problems while your spirit is dry and empty, you are only going to dry up even more.

It is time to stop. Get back into His presence. Top up. Then you will have more than enough to pour out to everybody around you.

CHAPTER 19

BECOMING A PROPHETIC MINISTER

CHAPTER 19 – BECOMING A PROPHETIC MINISTER

It's round about that time… that moment in time when the book is starting to wind down and I consider how many principles I can possibly fit into it before moving to the next book. However, seeing as though this is the last book of the *Prophetic Field Guide Series*, I am going to finish off strong!

I am going to take you through some practical ministry steps. As the Lord leads you into prophetic office, there are a couple of things that are going to change. Doors that were closed will open up again. Ministry visions that died are going to be resurrected.

I want to make sure that you are ready for it. So as you have gone through the process and increased the vessel you are and are enabled to pour out more anointing than ever… let me teach you how to use it properly!

The next two chapters are going to cover a 12 step program that is fit for any minister. As the Lord Jesus appoints you to prophetic office, you stand in a position of leadership position that requires a new level of responsibility.

These chapters will ensure that when you feel that weight on your shoulders, that you walk it out accordingly.

THE 12 STEP PROGRAM

Romans 12:6-15

> *6 Having then gifts differing according to the grace that is given to us, let us use them: if prophecy, let us prophesy in proportion to our faith;*
> *7 or ministry, let us use it in our ministering; he who teaches, in teaching;*
> *8 he who exhorts, in exhortation; he who gives, with liberality; he who leads, with diligence; he who shows mercy, with cheerfulness.*
> *9 Let love be without hypocrisy. Abhor what is evil. Cling to what is good.*
> *10 Be kindly affectionate to one another with brotherly love, in honor giving preference to one another;*
> *11 not lagging in diligence, fervent in spirit, serving the Lord;*
> *12 rejoicing in hope, patient in tribulation, continuing steadfastly in prayer;*
> *13 distributing to the needs of the saints, given to hospitality.*
> *14 Bless those who persecute you; bless and do not curse.*
> *15 Rejoice with those who rejoice, and weep with those who weep.*

1. IF PROPHECY, ACCORDING TO THE PROPORTION OF FAITH

> *6 Having then gifts differing according to the grace that is given to us, let us use them: if prophecy, let us prophesy in proportion to our faith;*

The first step is to get revelation. Do not head out on head knowledge, on past experiences, or past counseling cases. Every person is unique and wonderfully made.

You need to make sure that you get revelation for them. Just because you shared the gospel with someone and you led them to the Lord and it worked, does not mean that the exact same revelation is going to work for someone else.

You always need to go in humble, empty, and hungry saying, "Lord, what do you want me to share? What is your word for this person? I do not want to give them my word or my idea."

When you do this, you will get a Urim or a Thummim. When you are ministering, something will start to flow. You will find yourself saying things like, "You felt this and that in your heart, but God wants you to know that He has His hand on you and He is calling you to do this, this, and this."

Afterwards you will think, "I do not know where that came from."

The minute you engage, you need to get revelation. Say, "Lord, what do you want to say to this person?"

2. IN MINISTRY, TO MINISTER!

> *7 or ministry, let us use it in our ministering;*

Servanthood is ministry. Laying down your life is your role. You have to reach the person where they are at.

We often make this mistake in ministry. If you are in active ministry, you will know what I am talking about.

You try to get people to see things from your perspective, as if that will minister to them. It will not minister to them. You cannot make people see things through your eyes to meet their need.

You need to see things through their eyes to meet their need. If you are ministering to a child, you need to speak as a child. If you are ministering to someone that is in the world, try to connect to something that they can comprehend.

Take them from the known to the unknown. You cannot come speaking all of your terminology and then try to make them understand what you are saying, to minister to their need.

If they first have to study what you are saying before their need can be met, something is wrong! This is foolish. What does a servant do in the natural?

He looks at the needs of the master, right? He does things the master's way.

> **KEY PRINCIPLE**
>
> That is what it means to be in ministry. You do things the Master's way.

The Lord knows what that person needs. He knows the right words and things that you need to use to reach them. You cannot expect them to come into your church, abide by your church rules and your holiness living before you are prepared to share the truth with them.

Perhaps you have not noticed, but unbelievers and backsliders are in the world, not the church. (Well, it depends on what church you go to, but for the most part unbelievers are in the world.)

Do you think that by dragging them into your church or ministry that they will suddenly get healing? Yes, it happens, but someone would have had to notice, engage, and follow through with them in order for them to have even come to that meeting, right?

Someone had to reach them where they were at in the first place in order to get them to come to that meeting. You reach them on their terms for ministry, not on your own.

You need to go to where they are at with your language. You need to use the mindset and the archetype that they have and reach them there. Whether you like it or not, you need to do this or else you are not going to win them over and give them the truth that you have for them.

3. A TEACHER, IN TEACHING

> 7 ...*he who teaches, in teaching;*

This is no time for advice. People often confuse ministry and advice. Giving ministry is not about giving your good advice. I can call a hotline for that. I can say, "I am having a bad day, can you please give me advice?"

In fact, I can just walk through the mall with a small child. You will be amazed at how many people have so much advice. Fall pregnant, have a baby, or get married, and everybody will have advice for you.

> **KEY PRINCIPLE**
>
> Counsel is not about giving advice.
> Counsel is about teaching.

Stop saying, "I think." If you catch yourself saying, "I think," you are giving your advice. Counsel is given by the Word.

Counsel is not given on what you feel or what you think. Whenever you minister to someone, whether you got a word of revelation or whether you feel led to give them direction for their lives, that direction should always be based on the Word.

Sometimes the direction that you give them based on the Word does not line up with the direction that you would naturally give them. That is actually a good sign that you are flowing in the Spirit.

In the natural, you may advise them to do one thing, but in the spirit you may feel something completely different. The Word might even say something completely different.

So, put what you feel and think aside because counsel is about teaching. There is something about ministering by using Scripture. It gives you a back-up.

Not only does it have the power to set them free, but they also cannot come back to you and say, "You told me to do this. I did it and now my life is a mess."

You can say, "No, I did not tell you to do that. The Word of God told you to do that."

If you are going to give an instruction or say, "I think you should do this," then you need to base it on the Word.

You can tell someone that they need to love their brother and sister because the Word says, "He that does not love his brother, does not love the Lord."

It is very simple.

You should say, "No, I do not feel that you should get a divorce because Jesus Himself said that we should not divorce. Divorce is not of the Lord. Unless there has been a break in covenant, you are not entitled to that divorce."

Now, my advice is that he is really mean and I do not know how you, as a woman, can sit under such an unpleasant gentleman. I would kick his butt out of there. That is my advice.

However, the Word of God says that unless he has broken covenant, you have no grounds for divorce. Do you see how dangerous that one little point can be?

Let's stick to the Word of God here. That is our foundation. You would be amazed to see how much damage has been done to the Church from people giving advice like that.

People say, "Five prophets told me that I should divorce my husband."

Then, they divorce their husband and their lives are terrible and things are complicated. Then, do you know what that person ends up doing? They blame the prophets.

They blame God and say that He ruined their marriage and that the prophets told them to divorce their husband and it was wrong. They say, "Now my life is a mess and everything is crazy. I should not have done that. Everything has gone wrong."

God gets the blame. However, if we would just base everything on the Word, they could try to blame the Word all they would like, but then it is not your word against theirs. It is God's word against theirs.

Keep yourself on a secure foundation. Do not get caught up. If you are going to give advice, because you cannot help yourself, then do what Apostle Paul does.

Say, "Guys, this is what I am telling you, not the Lord - me. This is what I am saying regarding being single. I think that you should just stay single. However, know that this is not a command from the Lord. This is just my advice."

If you are going to give your advice, make sure that they know that it is your advice and that they can choose to receive it or not. When it is the Word of God, you can say, "This is the Word of God and you better listen."

4. IF AN ENCOURAGER, IN EXHORTATION

> *8 he who exhorts, in exhortation;*

> **KEY PRINCIPLE**
>
> When you engage someone in ministry, you always need to give them hope.

You need to let them know what the picture is going to look like on the other side.

It is like this, they come to you for marital counsel because they are fighting like mad. The first thing that you want to do is paint a good picture of what a marriage looks like.

You say, "You know what guys? The Lord is going to use the two of you as a powerful team. I see that He is going to use you for a very specific purpose.

I see you stepping out as one and being a leadership team, being used of the Lord, being in love, and having a marriage that is an example for others to follow."

Give them that picture in their heart first. Once they have a picture in their hearts, they will be prepared to deal with whatever else they need to deal with in order to reach that goal.

However, if they just see their sin, their failures, and everything that is going to go wrong, without any hope, why should they go through that change?

Why should they go through death after death, deal with their sin, or let go of their bad habits, just because the Word says so?

Some people will do it out of their pure love for the Lord, however, for most people, they need a little bit more than that. They need hope. They need a reason to go through and to keep hanging on. They need a reason to obey the Word.

You would think that salvation would be enough, but if you have worked with people, you already know that I do not need to press that point. Even you need hope, so what do you think about the person that you are ministering to?

Start out by giving them a picture of what the good stuff looks like at the end. Then, start taking them through the process.

5. One That Gives, With Generosity

> *8 ...he who gives, with liberality*

Before you engage, know that it is going to cost you.

> **Luke 9:62** *And Jesus said to him, "No one, having put his hand to the plow, and looking back, is fit for the kingdom of God."*

Do not think that you can do a "drive by ministry session." If you are going to engage with someone, you have to follow through until the end.

That means, are you prepared to give your time, love, money, and whatever else it takes to meet that need and see that person through? If you are not, do not even begin.

You can just sit in your little room thinking about doing ministry one day, because if you are not prepared to follow through with someone, then you have no starting point.

You cannot go halfway through a ministry session and say, "I do not like how this person is spewing at me. I do not like their attitude right now. I am out of here."

It is going to get messy. They are going to spew and spit. It is going to get ugly. Are you prepared to follow through? Do you have what it takes to handle all that stuff being splattered in your face? Because it is coming!

You are going to touch on sensitive places that they do not want to hear about. What do you think is going to happen when you say, "So, what have you done in your marriage to make it fail?"

Do you think that you are not going to have something coming back at you, when you say that?

You are going to have to say, "What wrong did you do in this conflict between you and your sister? Where is your sin?"

How many people are happy to hear, "You have a root of bitterness in your life. You have a law of judgment here. It is your sin that has led you to this point. Are you ready to deal with it?"

Not everyone likes to hear that. Are you prepared to face the rejection? If you are not, do not go there in the first place because you are going to do more harm than good.

You are going to cut them open and then leave them like that on the operating table.

6. ONE THAT RULES, WITH DILIGENCE;

> *8 ... he who leads, with diligence*

Take charge of the ministry session. Do not let them lead. You need to lead. It is a bit of a contradiction because on one hand you are there as a servant and to meet their need, but on the other hand, there comes a time when you have to step in and lead the conversation to make sure that it goes where God wants it to go.

For example, let's say that you are helping someone break free of bitterness towards their father. You engage, they start sharing their story, you get revelation, and then the next thing you know, they start going off on this whole tangent that leads the conversation away from the point that you know the Lord is trying to make, which is to deal with the bondage in their lives that is rooted in this bitterness.

If you let them go on for too long, you are going to lose the anointing and your opportunity. You have to know when to step in and steer the conversation in the right direction.

Take charge. You are the minister. You need to create the environment that they need in order to follow through. If you are ministering inner healing with someone to the hurts of the past, they can really talk for hours and hours.

It is good to let them talk for a bit, but then there comes a time when they have had enough time to spew bitterness and then it is time to get to the root of the problem.

If you just let them spew and spew for hours and think that is ministry, then you may as well put a sign on your door, start charging, and call yourself a psychologist, because even the world does that. Why bother?

You can sit on the couch and spew bitterness at me for an hour and I just say, "Shame. Your mother was mean. I understand. You had it bad."

"Praise you Lord. Thank you for my sister. I pray that she has a good week. Amen."

That is not ministry. That is psychology. You may as well send them to the world. What is the point of you ministering to them? You need to take charge and lead them.

You need to say, "I see that you have bitterness there."

"No, I do not."

"Really? Did you not hear what you just said? Do you not feel what is in your heart right now? Let's go there."

You need to start asking them questions and directing the conversation. You can say, "I sense something there. Tell me a bit more about that. Do you sense that bitterness? Do you see what happened in your life at this time?"

Then, once they start pouring out, you can lead them and you can pray for inner healing. You can say, "I see a picture of you at this age. I see something demonic. I feel that you need to apply this scripture to your life…"

You need to take charge and lead them. Give them the liberty to share, but do not be afraid to lead them to conviction.

7. One That Shows Compassion, With Cheerfulness.

> *8 ...he who shows mercy, with cheerfulness.*

I teach my children these two words when ministering, "I understand." That does not mean I accept, it means I understand. You cannot say to someone, "I know exactly how it feels."

You do not know exactly how it feels. You are not them. You did not have their upbringing and you did not experience their exact case scenario. You may have had something similar, but you cannot say, "I know exactly how it feels."

However, you can say, "I understand." Those two words, I understand, show more compassion than anything else because it lets them know that you acknowledge that they have had a bad experience.

It also lets them know that you are there to help them through it. Even if they are spewing and carrying on, they just need one person in this world to say, "I understand."

These two words can minister more than anything else, especially when you are hurting and frustrated and feel like nobody cares.

8. Let Love be Sincere.

9 Let love be without hypocrisy.

This is not one of those things where you can "fake it until you make it." Perhaps you have not realized this yet, but you cannot love like this in the natural.

You need the agape love of the Lord to be able to love in this way. This is just point eight and I guarantee that you are saying, "I have messed up on every single one of these at least once in my life. Am I ever going to get it right?"

It is called ministry, not psychoanalysis. It is a spiritual principle. You cannot gain ministry naturally. You cannot drum up and squeeze out agape love.

You cannot somehow find it in your toes and just squeeze it out. It is spiritually discerned - a fruit of the spirit. You need to tap into your spirit and receive agape love from the Lord.

Actually, it is good when you hit your limitations and when you mess up all these points because you realize that if the Lord does not step in and give you what you need, you are doing it all on personality power.

That is why I am making these points so clear, because how much ministry do you see being done on personality power? Everyone is saying, "I feel, I think, I sense, I assume, and I determine."

Then, they quickly find a scripture to back up all those things. They do it without any real revelation or love and without leading you to real victory. They just throw the problem at you and let you stew in it while they walk away.

Let's not find ourselves caught in that same rut of trying to minister to God's people with personality power. You are just going to come to the point of realizing that you did not have as much personality power as you thought you had.

Sooner or later, you are going to get drained, and you are going to say, "The work of the ministry is exhausting." That is when you do it with personality power.

If you do it in your own flesh, it is terribly exhausting. However, if you do it with the Spirit of God, as you empty, He pours in and fills you up.

It is actually the most draining, not when you are being used of God, but when you are trying to use yourself.

You are trying to empty out your own vessel with your own power. You are trying to be your own Holy Spirit and for everyone else out there.

If you go through a ministry time and you are absolutely drained, either you did not follow through, you were not led, or you just poured out of your soul, instead of your spirit.

Our agape love has to be sincere, it has to be the real deal. It cannot just be about you having a specific personality that you have had your whole life. It has to be something that God gives you.

That is why I said that it is the nature of the born again, child of God. It is not the nature of man to be nice to people. Ministry is a lot more than just being nice.

9. Abhor What Is Evil; Be Joined to What Is Good.

9 ...Abhor what is evil. Cling to what is good.

Just because you have sincere love and compassion, it does not mean that you have to accept sin. Sin is sin. God hates sin and so should you. Do not be afraid to address sin. Be firm and do not back down regarding sin, especially if they are open to ministry.

If they got that picture of the goal and they really want the blessing of the Lord, then you have to say, "Ok, if you want that blessing and you want to reach that goal, then you are going to have to give up certain sins."

For example, if you are having trouble in your marriage, as a husband, perhaps you need to start putting your wife and family first, instead of your job.

You need to give something up because you are neglecting what God has given you.

If you are a wife, perhaps you are so busy running around getting your need met everywhere else that you are not being there for your husband when he needs you.

That is sin. You are not submitting to his covering. If you want the perfect marriage, are you prepared to pay the price? The price that you have to pay is your sin.

Abhor the sin, but love the person. Do not just love on them and love on them and think that this alone will bring victory. If you want to see the Father loving on Jesus, then look at the cross.

That is what it looks like for someone to be loved on. Love is not sitting there listening to someone share all of their problems and saying, "Shame, shame."

That is not ministry. That is psychology. That is a support group. You may as well go out and join one of those support groups.

"Hi, my name is Colette."

Everyone replies together, "Hello, Colette."

The world has that down. We do not need to compete. Let's get rid of the support groups and start doing some real ministry in the kingdom of God.

That means not being afraid to say, "You have a problem with alcohol. Let's deal with that demon."

"Adultery is a sin. Let's bring you to repentance. Your bitterness is sin. The fact that you do not love your brother and that you are in conflict and strife is sin. Your homosexuality is sin."

Now, I cannot say, "It is sin" and then run out the back door. I am going to have sincere love and compassion. I am going to say, "It is sin, but I understand."

"I know that you have had one tough life, but I am taking you by the hand and we are going to go through this. We are going through together, until you have the victory.

We are going to keep going until you do not need a drink anymore. I am not leaving your side until we have the victory. I do not care if we have to go and find another pastor or pray every day. We are seeing this thing through."

That is ministry. You see the sin and still have the courage to stick through with them, until they get the victory. If you did this, people would be more open to share their sin with you.

On the other hand, do not think that just saying nice words and saying, "I understand" will make the sin suddenly go away.

You say, "Love will overcome all."

Yes, it will. However, your definition of love and the Word's definition of love is not the same thing because love is not "nice". Love is very active and very sharp. It is an even greater force than faith and hope.

10. BE AFFECTIONATE, PUTTING OTHERS FIRST

10 Be kindly affectionate to one another with brotherly love, in honor giving preference to one another;

This one follows the previous point so beautifully, because after you have seen their sin, it can get nasty. Perhaps you have had it where you go to address bitterness or a sin, and then they turn around and pull out all of your mistakes?

"Well, if you were just a better leader, maybe I would feel comfortable opening up to you. If you did not let me down, then I might have received the word that you had from God."

They may even say, "Are you really pointing that sin out in me?

Who gives you the right to talk to me like that?

I am hearing something completely different from God right now.

You are just being controlling and putting me down. Why do I have to listen to you?"

Nope – you are not the only one who has faced this in ministry!

The decision that you make in this moment will make or break your ministry as a whole. That is why I love this point. You need to lead the way by putting others first.

This is where you learn to get yourself out of the way. When you start hitting on people's hurts, it is going to get ugly. There are certain things that they are going to say that will make your toes curl.

They are going to make you feel insecure and there will be a temptation to stop in that moment and say, "Maybe I said that too harshly. It is true, I really am a bad leader.

I made a mistake. I should not have said that to them over there. I should not have lost my temper."

What did you just do? You stopped ministering. You took your eyes off them and put them on yourself. Do not do it. When they start spewing and there are ugly things being said and they are carrying on, you need to put yourself aside.

In that moment, I always feel like I take all of my hurts, feelings, and all those things that would ordinarily be offensive to me and I just tuck them into a little box and put it next to me in the room.

That is the best way that I can describe how I do this. I look at them objectively and I say, "Why do you say that? Then, what did I say and what did I do? Good, give me more."

You know how the matador has a red flag and he puts it out in front of the bull and says, "Come on, bull?"

The bull gets so angry. It glares at the matador, "Do not flick that flag at me."

The matador says, "Give me your best shot."

The bull dashes for the flag and the matador steps out of the way saying, "Come on, bull. Is that all you've got?"

That is how you need to be during ministry. "Get it out. Get it all out. Is that all you have to say?"

Eventually the bull will get tired, but you are going to exhaust yourself more, if you do not step out of the way.

You have to step out of the way. Do not step in the way of the bull or hold the flag in front of your face. Step aside. Do not get emotionally involved right now.

This is not about your emotion. It is about theirs. Once you are done and the bull is nice and calm and you have ministered, then you can go home, cry on your pillow and have your spouse or team minister to you.

That is when you can pull open that box of yours and fall apart. However, it is not time to fall apart in the middle of ministering to someone. It is not time to defend yourself or to deal with your sin. Deal with that later.

Right now, you need to address their sin. Put yourself aside and your feelings aside and say, "Why did you say that? What is it about that that made you so mad?

Why do you say that I am controlling? What do you feel right now? What is coming up from inside of you? Who else treated you that way? Why are you responding like this right now?

What if I told you to do something you do not want to hear? What does that bring out of you?

Now, tell me what you are feeling and how you are responding right now, do you feel that this is in line with the Word of God? Do you feel that you are justified and that you are responding righteously in this situation?

No? Why not?

You need to bring them to conviction. They will start to realize that they are overreacting just a little bit. Then, you can say, "Good. Let me show you what is happening.

This started at a certain age and you responded badly. I know that you are mad at your spouse right now or at what is going on at work, but spewing at me is not going to make the problem go away."

We need to go back to the source of the problem and bring victory. Those are some of the best ministry times that you can have and some of the greatest breakthroughs.

In fact, be grateful if they spew and carry on. You have a live wire. You can work with that. That also means that all the hurt is on the outside and you do not have to go digging to find it.

11. REJOICING IN HOPE; PERSEVERING UNDER PRESSURE; CONTINUALLY IN PRAYER;

> *12 rejoicing in hope, patient in tribulation, continuing steadfastly in prayer;*

Do not give up. I know how discouraging it can be sometimes, especially when you minister to the same person about the same problem again and again.

You say, "Lord, help me. I want to hurt them. How many more times must I say the same thing before they finally get the memo and realize that they need to stop being bitter?"

They say, "I need to put myself aside and let God be in control."

"Yes, it has been ten years. Can we do that now?"

It can be discouraging when you are ministering to the same person with the same problem. However, God never gave up on you. No matter how discouraging it gets, why don't you have more faith in them than they have in themselves?

> **KEY PRINCIPLE**
>
> Expect them to break free, not because they are so great, but because the Holy Spirit is so great and He is able to meet every single need.

He will push through with them, so you should push through with them.

Always have positive expectation and leave the solution and answer up to the Lord. You just need to expect the best and leave the end result up to the Lord.

12. REJOICE WITH THOSE THAT REJOICE. WEEP WITH THOSE THAT WEEP.

> *15 Rejoice with those who rejoice, and weep with those who weep.*

Doesn't this beautiful verse sum up the entire chapter? Sharing one another's infirmities, taking time to notice needs, taking time to engage, taking time to follow through, and taking time to follow up.

Once you have led someone through this process and you have helped them in ministry, follow up. If you led someone to the Lord, follow them up, visit with them.

If you ministered to someone regarding their marriage, give them a call and ask them how their marriage is doing. Do not just minister and run. Follow up and continue that relationship.

It will open other doors. If they are struggling, give them a project to do. Do not give up. Press through. This is the work, the labor of ministry. This is not the dance or the "walk through the park" of ministry.

This is the work of the ministry and it is meant to cost us. That is why it is a calling and that is why it is spiritual. We cannot do this in ourselves.

CHAPTER 20

PROPHETIC COUNSELING: INNER HEALING

Chapter 20 – Prophetic Counseling: Inner Healing

I love to see the look on the face of our prophetic students that start heading towards prophetic office and I drop the bombshell… now it is time to learn to be a pastor.

Ah yes, if looks could spit, I would be surfing. Prophets do not like being told to be pastors. I have already hinted at this already, so let's dive headlong into this reality.

> **Key Principle**
>
> From the time you are placed in prophetic office, to perfectly fulfill your purpose, you need to learn some pastoral ministry.

Now I am not talking about becoming a pastor in a local church. The office of the pastor is two-fold. Refer to *Today's Pastor* if you want to understand that a bit better. Rather I am talking about the ministry aspect of the pastor.

It is the anointing and function that the shepherd is called to, to take care of the sheep. There is no use having all that anointing and power and no practical way to walk it out.

Even in the previous chapters as I gave you instruction on how to minister, you should have got the hint! To do this kind of ministry... you need to be a pastor.

I will let you in on a secret. To train the prophets, you need to be a good prophetic pastor. Does that sound crazy? Not at all, because if there was ever one of the fivefold that needed the gentle touch of the pastor... it is the prophet.

They have a sharp edge and sure do not mince their words, but are not so good at receiving it back in the same way that they hand it out. Hurts of the past and rejections make them a tad... sensitive!

Regardless of whether you are ministering to a fellow prophet or someone that has recently got born again, you need to start growing up in your calling. As you stand in prophetic office, your ministry needs to mature and you need to "fill out," spiritually speaking.

Maturity is going to require becoming a leader and a pastor - both will be used as vehicles for your prophetic anointing!

This entire chapter is dedicated to the prophetic pastor... or is it the pastoral prophet... I tell you what – you decide!

THE PASTORAL PROPHET

Now the way that a prophet counsels is quite different to pastoral ministry. You are not just going to teach them - you are going to counsel them prophetically.

That's a bit what I am going to take you through in this chapter. I am going to give you some practical pointers on how to minister prophetically.

It is one thing to get revelation during intercession, but it is another one when someone comes to you for healing or help with a spiritual blockage.

In *Prophetic Warrior* and *Prophetic Counter Insurgence*, I taught you how to deal with somebody when they have a demonic bondage. I gave you pointers on how to deal with curses and for the most part you understand the process. Simple, right? We get revelation.

However, counseling and receiving prophetic revelation are not the same thing. What do you say when someone comes to you with a marital problem or their son is in rebellion? Getting a revelation will only take you so far. You need to give them more than a "thus saith the Lord." You need to give them practical help that they can use for the situation.

Do you keep getting revelation for someone, but they keep coming back to you with the same problem? Make note of this: Spiritual revelation does not make problems go away!

Consider revelation like a spotlight. Remember what you learned about prophetic decree in the *Prophetic Essentials*? You learned that until you spoke forth the vision, that nothing would come to pass. Well the same applies in prophetic counseling, except it is going to take more than just speaking forth the revelation this time.

Now you need to learn to apply it effectively. This is more part of your calling than you realize. The ministry of inner healing is one of the core functions of the prophet – although you would not think so if you met many prophets.

They like to send "broken people" for pastoral counseling or to the "deliverance team." Do *not* get me started on that! If there was ever a fivefold ministry to which the broken should be sent... it is the prophet!

Don't you realize that the Lord has given you a heart to feel with the broken? What do you think He gave that to you for? Now it is all making sense isn't it? Everything I shared about the brokenness in becoming the image of Jesus starts to find its way to resurrection.

There is no greater power than feeling the hurt of the hurting and then reaching out with the healing that will change their lives. Now everything you learned and have become is blended into the perfect picture.

You feel their hurt. You see the source of it. You flow in the anointing to heal it. Now all that you need to do, is follow that through with practical ministry and... what do you know... you are being a prophet.

As the Lord begins opening doors for ministry again, I want you to remember that many things have changed. You are not the same person you were. Know that you are in a place to start bringing real change in God's people.

Real Problems Require Real Counsel

> ***Psalms 147:3*** *He heals the brokenhearted and binds up their wounds.*

They need counsel. A real problem needs some tangible one-on-one ministry. Although you and a pastor-teacher will both counsel and even flow in the same gifts of the spirit, the way that you operate will be different. The anointing that you operate in will be decidedly different!

So, I am going to teach you how a prophet counsels. I want to take you through this process a step at a time. I am keeping this really simple and giving you just four steps that you need to follow.

So, as you are coming now to the end of this book, and instead of feeling more like a prophet, you keep feeling Him lead you to pastor His sheep… relax! Your entire journey has been preparing you for this. Now is the time to take the prophetic anointing and to stretch yourself as you step into the Church.

Spoiler Alert: Leadership Training Ahead

You are right where God needs you to be. When you make the transition to prophetic office, you are going to find something interesting happens – your leadership will be taken up a notch.

You have learned to flow in the gifs. You have learned to become a prophet. The Lord has dealt with your preconceived ideas. He has taken you through deception. You know how to engage in spiritual warfare. You have become the vessel that God needs you to be.

But, you need to be and do more than that. You actually need to take that vessel and do the work of the ministry with it, just like I taught you in the previous chapter. To accomplish the work of the ministry means to work with people.

It means taking all your experience and everything that you have lived and done, and begin helping people break free.

Don't think that you are a prophet just so you can train up other prophets. Maybe, that is one of your functions. But, that's not even the beginning of all that God has called you to do.

It is like people who are professional students. All they are ever good for is to teach others everything they know. They never do anything with their years of study.

Didn't you just hate those highly intellectual algebra teachers at school? What could they really accomplish in real life besides teaching other people their knowledge?

I don't know about you, but I certainly don't want to be one of those. I want to do something with what God has given me. I want to use that math to make generators and change the world! In the same way, don't you want to do something with all that anointing?

THE FIVE STEP COUNSELING PROCESS

Unless you become a better leader, you are not going to mature. Nobody is going to receive from you.

One important part of being in prophetic office is being able to counsel and to help people through their day-to-day problems.

You need to know before you head out, that you cannot do any of this without the anointing. The rest of this chapter is the practical use, if you will, of prophetic office.

STEP 1: LISTEN

How profound, right? It is more profound than you think, because nobody ever does it! Think about the last time you had a problem. How many people really listened to you before interrupting you with "advice"?

Perhaps they heard you, but did they listen? Did they listen to the things that you did say? Did they listen to the things that you didn't say? Did they care enough to notice?

Step 1 for counseling is to stop and listen. Don't go in there with your preconceived ideas, assuming you already have the answer. You don't have the answer yet.

You don't understand where they are at. This is their problem and this is their life – not yours.

Do Not Underestimate Matters of the Heart

No matter how trivial it may seem to you, their problem is very real to them. Don't ever underestimate a person's problem. It might seem insignificant to you, but to them, it is very real. Often when we look at the problems of others, we consider how we would handle them.

In our minds, it is not a big deal. So you don't have finances? Trust God! So you are sick? Pray! So your husband is abusive? Submit or leave him! Sounds so simple doesn't it... until you are in those situations.

In the moments when your heart is torn in two and all the foundations of the past keep reminding you that you are a failure and will end up just like your mother... that problem is a Goliath in your life! Do not underestimate matters of the heart.

That's why you have to listen. Get yourself out of the way. Put your blind spot out of the way and listen to them.

Step 2: Expose the Real Problem: Ask Questions

Now not everyone knows how to properly express their problem. All they usually feel is their hurt or frustration, so you are going to need to help a little bit.

Here is something you need to keep in mind when counseling. As a prophet, it is likely that the Lord will begin giving you revelation the moment they begin sharing. Your first temptation will be to interrupt them and "deal with the problem." Resist that temptation! You see, until they can see their problem for themselves, you are wasting your time!

So they need to hear themselves express that problem. You could tell them what their problem is, or you could ask them some questions that help them vocalize that problem. There is quite a lot of power in hearing your own voice express the core of your problem.

For example, say for example a woman comes to you for counsel about her marriage. She wants to serve the Lord and her husband is digging in his heels – refusing to move forward in the Lord.

She begins to tell you everything he has done to hinder her. How hard it is to serve the Lord and how it is destroying her love and call. A well-placed question helps bring perspective:

"So are you saying that your problem is that you cannot love or serve the Lord, because your husband does not want to love or serve the Lord?"

"Are you saying that if your husband was not in your life, that you could flow in the anointing?

"Are you saying that if you had a different family, that you would not have the problems you do right now?

Anyone with a real heart for God will think twice about that, because no matter what her husband does, he can never take away her ability to love the Lord!

Of course that is not the problem! The problem runs a lot deeper than that, but most people do not see the problem! They need to sort through all those "feelings" and "triggers" and look into their own heart. You can help the process along by asking these three questions:

THE THREE QUESTIONS

1. What is your problem?
2. What have you done to solve this problem?
3. What would you like me to do about this problem?

You see, the third one is important because they might just want you to listen and not want any advice at all.

Notice that the question does not ask "who is the problem", but "what is the problem". Get them looking at themselves as soon as possible.

"Oh, my husband, he cares more for his work than he does for me."

"So, what is the problem?"

"Can't you see? He doesn't love me as he should…"

"But, what's the problem?"

"The problem is that I am bitter at him." Okay, now we have a problem that we can solve!

STEP 3: COUNSEL THE PERSON IN FRONT OF YOU

You see, you cannot fix somebody that is not in front of you! You will read this chapter again and again because it is going to save you stomach ulcers. Trust me!

You cannot counsel somebody who is not present. So you cannot counsel a husband that is at work, while his wife is sitting in front of you.

A husband lays out everything his wife does to him. Are you going to start addressing his wife? He is right, his wife should submit and she should honor him. There is just one little catch… the wife is not the one who came for counsel! His wife is sitting at home.

So, who are you going to address? For those who come to me for counsel, (just so you are warned ahead of time) I don't care if you have the worst husband in the world and he is completely in the wrong. If you came to me alone for marital counsel, know now who I am going to address – you! I can't address your husband because he is not there.

Even if I agree with you, I still have to deal with your problem. Otherwise, what do you go away with? "Yes, it's just as I thought, my husband is the reason for every problem in my life." That doesn't give you any hope. That doesn't give you a solution.

LOOK OUT FOR TEMPLATES AND TRIGGERS

If someone comes to you with feelings that they cannot control, it is quite likely you are looking at a trigger.

Remember your *Prophetic Boot Camp* phase? You were triggering all over the place! Now you can use everything you learned there and apply it to the person in front of you. By now, you should know very well what a trigger looks like!

Ask, "When did this problem start? Around what time?" That just really starts painting a picture. It starts painting a picture of where the problem began. You can look for triggers.

If you feel you need more, sign up for our *Pastor Teacher School* for more training on in-depth counseling. For now, I am giving you enough to get you headed in the right direction!

*TAKE NOTE: S*IN IS *K*NOCKING AT THE *D*OOR

So you have the steps down. You have listened and you have asked your questions. The problem is starting to become clear.

Never forget though that the root of every problem and the cause of every problem in life is... sin.

When you have that clear, you realize that it is that person that you are addressing. You are not addressing their husband, their wife, their children, their grandparents, or what their mother did to them twenty years ago. Rather, you are addressing... them.

You can't even bring healing to those memories until you have dealt with their sin and their sinful response to those circumstances.

> **KEY PRINCIPLE**
>
> It is not what life does to us that makes us who we are, but it is how we respond to what life does to us that defines us.

So listen, but never forget that you have to deal with something sooner or later. You are going to have to address that sin sooner or later. Listen for it. Listen for the fear. Listen for the bitterness. Listen for the guilt. Listen for whatever is coming up.

"When did this problem start?"

"What is the problem?"

"How do you feel?"

Get them to share and… listen!

Once they have spilled their heart on the floor, then it is time to take this to the Lord. You see, you don't jump in there and say, "Well, I see what your problem is." No, that's not the time!

You see, you are not a pastor-teacher, you are a prophet. A pastor-teacher can take the scriptures and say, "Okay, this is what your problem is…" But, you are not a pastor-teacher, you are pastoral prophet or a prophetic pastor… feel free to label yourself with what makes you happy! (Yes people... hear the sarcasm in my tone. Come now... you know me by now and can hear that edge of humor in my voice. We have got to know each other pretty well over the last couple of books, haven't we?)

STEP 4: GET REVELATION

So that's what you are going to do. Get revelation. You have listened to their problem and your mind is all over the place. If fact, according to every principle that you have learned so far, this problem could be a hundred different things. You add in your own feelings, experience, and everything you know... only to tie yourself up in knots.

I tell you what - just don't do it! Avoid the temptation to overthink this and rather go straight to getting revelation. After hearing so many different stories, you are going to pray and the Lord is going to give you revelation of where the real problem is.

This is what makes prophetic counseling rock! It's very powerful because you can cut through all of the garbage and stick your finger right on the main point of the problem.

You spend hours listening to all their problems and in just a few minutes, the Lord will sort through all of that and put His finger on what the real problem is!

TAKE NOTE: DON'T OVER LISTEN!

Now I know I have drummed the "listen to people" principle into your head and it is not a bad idea to go overboard on that as you are starting out. However, do not end up listening to someone for five hours before going to prayer.

All that is happening is that they are spewing all their poison and bitterness on you and instead of helping, you are going to walk away feeling spiritually drained and contaminated! Listen until you feel you have a good handle on the core of what they are going through. Then go to prayer.

INNER HEALING

After someone has shared their heart with me and then we go to prayer, the Lord will give me revelation according to where the person is right now. The revelation He will share will relate to the real problem. Avoid the temptation to get revelation about a problem you know they have, but have not shared yet!

Stick to what they came to you for. For example, if they came to you for marital counsel, now is not the time to pray about their conflicts with their pastor!

Now is the time that the Lord will zero in on the point and you will see various things.

If you see the person at a certain age, you can be sure that there is a hurt from the past that is affecting them right now.

Sometimes though you think that someone has a hurt from the past and you pray, only to see a demon attacking them! So never assume anything until you have come to pray.

For those that are broken and hurting though, you will likely see them at a certain age or see an event of the past that started the ball rolling, so to speak. This is the source of their problem.

This is where their bitterness began. This is where the hurt was formed. This is where you begin becoming the prophetic counselor that God has called you to be.

You will get revelations according to the source of the problem. You might see a chain in the spirit linking them to a parent – this speaks of a generational bondage.

There have been times when I saw a serpent wrapped around somebody's neck, which speaks of a spirit of deception. This means that the enemy has been lying to them.

There are other times when the Lord will show me a deep root of bitterness. I will say, "I see this deep root of bitterness."

I suggest referring back to the *Dreams and Visions Symbol Dictionary*, if you are not sure about the things you keep seeing while counseling.

A Full Circle

Look at that! We are at the end of this series, and I am taking you right to the beginning again of what you learned about dreams and visions. You have been forged into a vessel with a foundation you are going to use over and over again.

Don't think that because you are coming to the end of this entire series that that's it. No, you are going to live these principles repeatedly at deeper levels.

I taught you in *Prophetic Counter Insurgence*, how to help someone if they have a demonic bondage or curse in their lives.

I taught you in *Prophetic Boot Camp* how to minister inner healing. You learned how to deal with their sin and help them break free. Bring all of this together now, but realize it is going to be very different to what you have done up until now.

Until now, you have been in training… now you are stepping into office. This means a greater authority and expression of the anointing. Where you stumbled before, you will stand now. Where you were not sure before, you will see clearly now.

So do not end any counseling session until you have completed the final step!

Step 5: Follow up With Practicalities

Once you have listened, prayed, and brought healing, they still have to go home and face their husband or wife. They have to face their pastor and handle their boss. They still have to overcome the problem in their circumstance.

So, as they were sharing, you went to prayer and saw them at a certain age. You saw their father that said to them, "You will never amount to anything, you're stupid, you are just lazy."

So they just retreated into themselves. They didn't bother trying. You got the revelation, brought conviction to their bitterness and judgment of their father. You then spoke healing to their heart and dealt with any demonic bondages.

But you know, on Monday morning, they have to deal with that big boss that is always yelling at them and telling him that he is a failure, just as his father did. They return to the source of that trigger.

Making It Real

What are you going to do? You need to say, "Okay, now we have dealt with the spiritual problem, we need to deal with your habits now!"

"When you go to work on Monday, I want you to pour out in love to your boss. I want you to realize that you are there to be an asset to that company. I want you to start realizing that God has placed you there as a blessing and that you expect that company to be blessed."

"Start speaking blessing on your boss every moment you get. I want you to speak blessing on everything you do at work. Continually speak the blessing of God on everything you touch, expecting it to prosper."

You see, now you have given them something to do. Now that they have dealt with the spiritual side, they can deal with the habits as well. This final step is one of the most important because you can deal with all the spiritual stuff, but then they return to real life.

If you are operating in a fivefold ministry team, then I suggest hooking up with a pastor or teacher, especially for this part, because they will get revelation from the Word that can be applied daily.

When we minister as a team, I always team up a pastor with a prophet, because together they meet every need! The prophet gets revelation, convicts and brings healing. The pastor or teacher brings conviction through the Word, followed by practical counsel on how to walk it out.

Can you see why I said you need to work on your "pastoral side"? Still think you can do without it? This series is not called the "Pastoral Field Guide Series" though… but the *"Prophetic Field Guide Series"* so I will leave the teaching on counseling there and hopefully cause a hunger to grow in you to go even further in your call!

THIS IS REAL MINISTRY

Prophet... this is real ministry. I remember someone saying, "I always thought that ministry is standing behind the pulpit and preaching to the masses."

This is how you are going to change lives. A prophetic word comes and goes, but this kind of investment into the life of God's people lasts forever.

As you learn to counsel prophetically, you are going to grow and they are going to grow. This is what is going to happen when God brings you disciples or gives you a team.

Get ready for it. Don't think that disciples come already knowing what to do. If it is ever been on your heart to ask God that He brings you someone to be part of your team, then get ready to do this all the time.

In amongst all the things that are visible to the public, if you had to follow me home, this is what you would see all of the time. You would see me investing daily into my disciples and spiritual children.

Of all the messages I have preached behind the pulpit or books I have written, my heart will be found in the quiet of the counseling chamber as one of God's sheep lies broken before me, hungering for Jesus, needing help, needing a touch from Jesus and feeling so very far from it.

In this moment, I stand in the fullness of the prophet that He has called me to be. In this moment, as I see a heart healed, I understand my journey. The tears remind me of His scars and my heart beats with His.

This is the heart of Jesus for His bride. His love is found in the journey He has taken you through to shape and mold you, only to present you as an image of that love to a Church that desperately needs Him.

CHAPTER 21

APPOINTMENT TO PROPHETIC OFFICE

Chapter 21 – Appointment to Prophetic Office

You know, there is something about being appointed to any position. You put on the uniform, put on the badge, and you are transformed. When you look at yourself in the mirror you don't look the same way that you looked before, you don't act the same way you did before, and you don't even do the same things that you did before. Everything changes.

It is no different when it comes to being appointed to prophetic office. When you are appointed, the visions you had before will be no more, the way you did things will change, and the way you spoke is even going to change because you are not going to be the same person anymore. You are going to be a person of authority - you are going to be a leader in the kingdom of God.

Until you are prepared to come to that dividing place in your life to let go of the past, to let go of the image you were and be prepared to admit that God has something new for you, you will always stay in the old and remain limited.

Let me make it clear though, it is not the Lord who is limiting you. It's you who is limiting you.

THE NECESSITY OF LAYING ON OF HANDS

The Lord Jesus gave the fivefold ministry to the Body as a gift so that we might mature every single believer. So, it is the Lord Jesus who appoints the prophet to their place of authority. It comes with a decree and it comes with the laying on of hands by a fellow prophet or apostle.

You don't walk down the street and suddenly stand in prophetic office. You don't have a dream, and you are in prophetic office. You don't have a vision and a revelation where the Lord gives you a key and you are in prophetic office.

Jesus Christ, the Son of God, went to John the Baptist to be baptized by him. John said, "Lord, why should I baptize you?" He had seen the holy life that Jesus had lived. He figured, "What does this man need baptizing for? He has no sin." They were cousins and John knew Jesus well enough to see the kind of life He lived. (Matt 3:15)

The Lord said, "Let it be done so that all things might be complete." So Jesus got baptized. John the Baptist saw the dove come upon Jesus. That was the day, Jesus was appointed. That was the day, He was anointed for ministry. That was the day, He was placed in His position. From there He was led into the wilderness and only after that time of testing did His ministry begin.

Now, tell me something. If Jesus, who was the Son of God and perfect, needed a prophet to release Him, do you think you can get in on your own in your bedroom? Are you better than Christ?

Apostle Paul and Barnabas were set apart for the work of the ministry by laying of hand of the elders. Timothy was set apart by Paul. Joshua was set apart. Go through the scriptures. Even David was set apart by Samuel, and Solomon by David.

THROUGH THE AGENCY OF MAN

There always needs to be an agency of man. There always needs to be somebody else who is involved. You will see this pattern throughout the Word. If even these people needed some kind of release, then certainly you and I are no different. If Jesus Himself needed a prophet to release Him into His ministry, certainly you and I cannot boast anything more than that.

Without that appointment, you lack the authority that goes along with it. It would be like a man who tries to act like a police officer but has no badge to back up his position. You might act the part, but if you do not carry that seal, you do not have the authority.

WITHOUT THE AUTHORITY YOU ARE POWERLESS

When you speak the word of God, does it penetrate hearts to such a degree that it uproots, plants, tears down, builds up, and... brings change? That's the authority of the prophet. That's what prophetic office adds to you.

Appointment to Prophetic Office

It gives you the kind of authority that, when you put on your officer's uniform and hold your hand up high in the air, you can stop a truck dead in its tracks. That is prophetic authority.

What a theft is it to somebody who walks around saying, "I am in prophetic office" to make themselves feel good and then not have the authority to back that up.

Rather admit you have nothing. Rather admit you are not all the way there. That gives you an opportunity to climb higher into His presence and into His glory. That's what we need. We need more of that in the body of Christ.

What is it going to be? The choice is really yours! Are you going to follow through to the end? Are you going to pay the price? Are you going to pass the tests? If you are, then the Lord can do something for you. And He will put that prophetic authority on you.

MAKING THE TRANSITION

You are about to make the transition. You have been trained, challenged, and equipped. You have been stripped and then added to again. When you were at your weakest, He made you strong.

When you were the driest, He poured out His spirit on you. You are not qualified, because of your ability to hear His voice. You not are qualified because of your skill in prophecy.

Your qualification has come because you know how to say, "Lord, not my will, but yours be done."

You allowed the Roman soldiers to pierce you and you allowed the Lord Jesus to give you His heart. You allowed yourself to be nothing – taking the lower seat.

> **KEY PRINCIPLE**
>
> You finally understand that the power of the prophetic ministry is not held in your grand display, but in the force of your humility.

The authority does not lie in your emotional ranting, but in His tender touch.

When all is said and done, you will exchange your sword for oil. You will hand over the mighty rushing wind, for the gentle breeze of Jesus.

The mighty thunderstorm you were has become a refreshing summer rain. The hard edge has become satin and the clanging symbol a display of love.

Welcome prophet, you have finally come to the end of this part of your journey. Here, in the quiet, where no one can see your heart, you will understand, "Why you."

Don't you see? For all that God has done and all that He has taken from you, He desires to give you His greatest treasure ever - one that you can never earn. He has made you naked, so that He can clothe you with His love.

He has left you bleeding, so that very blood can heal His people. He took away the noise to fill you with a peace that passes understanding.

The Gentle Breeze of Jesus

You would think that after so much fire and travail that the power you stand in would be loud and release earthquakes. However, as you come to stand in office, realize that He is giving you something much more revolutionary. He is giving you a gentle breeze.

A love that rolls over the hearts of His people and heals their wounds. A breeze that ignites the flames that have died. A breeze that causes stony hearts to beat once again.

Do you want to see as much change as you talk about? Then the Bride needs to fall helplessly in love with her Savior. It is only in that moment that she will want to shed the weights that hold her back. It is only when we are consumed with love for Him that we will be willing to shed our sin and look at our failure.

When this hurting and dark world tastes the honey of His love, they will be satisfied. The craving will be met. Don't you understand that this is what God has called you to do?

Hear His Word for You Right Now

The honor of it washes over me as I write. Tears are lining my face as I look over this very long journey we have travelled together, because at each milestone, I see the face of Jesus looking down on us.

I see His hand beckoning us into the Throne Room. I see His glory and the power in His hand. I see His smile and hear His voice saying,

> *"Well done my good and faithful servant. Come rest with me for a while. Come and revel in my beauty for a while. For I have raised you up as an example in my Church.*
>
> *"I have raised you to sit in heavenly places and to reach out to my sheep and to remind them of who I am. Carry this scroll in your hand and send it out to all my people.*
>
> *"Let them know, 'Their King waits for them!' let them know, 'Their King longs for them.' Let them know that their King withholds nothing from them.*
>
> *For I have set a plan in motion. I have put you in place. I have put my heart in you and when you felt the most lost, I was making a way out of the darkness. When you were in the darkest sin, I was breathing on you to shake away the dross. When you were broken, bruised, and felt alone, I already made a plan to equip you to heal others.*

Come child. Become the vessel that I have shaped you for. I have made you as a vessel of honor, not because I found in you great skill and righteousness, but because I found in you a willing heart.

I found in you, a man after my own heart. I found in you, one that loves. So take these blessings from my hand, as I send you out now as a gift to my Church."

END NOTE – Where to From Here?

I am in awe of the journey we have travelled together, but I just want you to know… it has only begun. As you stand in prophetic office, the way opens up and you get to walk out all of these teachings.

From here, move on to the *Prophetic Mandate*. I wrote it especially for those who have reached prophetic office and now face the finality of that transition. There is so much more to being a prophet than you realize!

I am going to tell you a secret. When I first started writing this series I had a fear that I would be so repetitive, that I would be boring! I mean, how much could you possibly teach on the prophetic? Right?

As the journey unfolded, the Holy Spirit brought so much back to me. He caused me to relive every single principle. He filled me up and poured me out again. For hours, days, and weeks, at my desk, I wept until my shirt was drenched.

There were times that the anointing came on me so strongly, I felt as if I was in a cloud, not seeing or hearing anything else, other than what God was pouring out through me.

While writing some chapters in this series, there were times when I felt like the Holy Spirit picked me up and poured through me. I was reading as I was writing and standing in awe of receiving the principle, for the first time, myself. I was just the vessel – He was the author.

Colette Toach

With each step we took, the Lord revealed more of His heart for His Church and His passion for you – His prophet. My family kept me well supplied with tea, coffee and lunch. Otherwise I would just write through! How could I stop? At much as I poured out, I never experienced so much of His power.

When I wrote my first book *Practical Prophetic Ministry*, I put the entire book together in just 3 days. Taking teachings, I had done through the years and writing the bulk of new revelations, the Holy Spirit picked me up and poured me out.

This journey through *The Prophetic Field Guide Series* was a continuation of that. As I am penning the last words to the page, I am torn. On the one hand I am overwhelmed with so much emotion, having reached the end of this race. On the other, I feel the death in letting it go, because these teachings have shaped me as much as they have shaped you.

They have reminded me again and again, why I began this journey. My mind wanders to the 22-year-old girl, freshly placed in prophetic office. Naïve and foolish enough to think that all the Church needed to change was a reality of the love of Christ. Twenty years later, and He continues to remind me of the heart He gave me long ago.

I taught a message called, *Love – Empowered to Change* and in it, I teach how what you love shapes you. It shapes your character and the direction you take in life.

End Note

As I finalize this last paragraph, I am reminded again of that love. I want you to know that the love that has shaped me all these years is… the love I have for you. The prophet. The leader. The broken-hearted mighty warrior who has so much more to give the world than you realize. Now, let me pass on this baton to you. Let what you love shape and empower you also and may that love forever be for Jesus and His beautiful Bride.

ABOUT THE AUTHOR

Born in Bulawayo, Zimbabwe and raised in South Africa, Colette had a zeal to serve the Lord from a young age. Coming from a long line of Christian leaders and having grown up as a pastor's kid she is no stranger to the realities of ministry. Despite having to endure many hardships such as her parent's divorce, rejection, and poverty, she continues to follow after the Lord passionately. Overcoming these obstacles early in her life has built a foundation of compassion and desire to help others gain victory in their lives.

Since then, the Lord has led Colette, with her husband Craig Toach, to establish *Apostolic Movement International,* a ministry to train and minister to Christian leaders all over the world, where they share all the wisdom that the Lord has given them through each and every time they chose to walk through the refining fire in their personal lives, as well as in ministry.

In addition, Colette is a fantastic cook, an amazing mom to not only her 4 natural children, but to her numerous spiritual children all over the world. Colette is also a renowned author, mentor, trainer and a woman that has great taste in shoes! The scripture to "be all things to all men" definitely applies here, and the Lord keeps adding to that list of things each and every day.

About the Author

How does she do it all? Experience through every book and teaching the life of an apostle firsthand, and get the insight into how the call of God can make every aspect of your life an incredible adventure.

Read more at www.colette-toach.com

Connect with Colette Toach on Facebook!
www.facebook.com/ColetteToach

Check Colette out on Amazon.com at:
www.amazon.com/author/colettetoach

RECOMMENDATIONS BY THE AUTHOR

If you enjoyed this book, we know you will love the following on the prophetic.

PROPHETIC MANDATE

By Colette Toach

Everyone wants to be a prophet, but being a prophet is so much more than just prophesying and flowing in the gifts. It is a long road of training, dying to the flesh and being put in the fire again and again to become the vessel that the Lord desires you to be. But for those who actually survive the refining process and make it to prophetic office, what happens next?

If you have made it to prophetic office, it is merely the beginning of walking out your true purpose in the body of Christ to equip his people and help bring His bride to unity and maturity. Apostle Colette gives you all the details, insight and practical how-tos of what the Lord gives each and every prophet once they reach office: a mandate.

Do not let the price you have paid go to waste. Walk out your calling with all the power, anointing and authority the Lord has given you!

PROPHETIC ESSENTIALS

Book 1 of the Prophetic Field Guide Series

By Colette Toach

In this book, you will find out that the call of the prophet goes far deeper than the functions and duties that the prophet fulfills. Anyone flowing in prophetic ministry can carry out tasks similar to the prophet.

If it burns in you to pay any price that is necessary and to stand up and break down the barriers between the Lord Jesus and His Bride, then my friend, you have picked up the right tool that will confirm the fire in your belly and the call of God on your life.

PROPHETIC FUNCTIONS

Book 2 of the Prophetic Field Guide Series

By Colette Toach

There is so much more to the prophet than standing up in church and prophesying.

Laid out beautifully so that you can understand and relate, Colette shares from her own personal experiences. Be prepared to live and experience the Lord like never before. This is not fiction… this is your training guide to the prophetic.

PROPHETIC ANOINTING

Book 3 of the Prophetic Field Guide Series

By Colette Toach

God has promised you a visit to the throne room! This is your summons from Almighty God. It is time for you to experience Him face-to-face and heart-to-heart.

Get ready for the meeting of a lifetime. The veils that have hindered the anointing in your life are going to be ripped away, and you are going to shine with His glory in every area of your life.

PROPHETIC BOOT CAMP

Book 4 of the Prophetic Field Guide Series

By Colette Toach

For it is in the training of the prophet that he begins to realize that all of His scrapes and bruises along the way are the very thing that the people will be able to identify with.

So, prophet of God, are you ready to sign up for boot camp? The Holy Spirit will be your sergeant and this book will be your training manual! Together you will be shaped, challenged, inspired and in the end, equipped to stand as a prophet in office.

PROPHETIC WARRIOR

Book 5 of the Prophetic Field Guide Series

By Colette Toach

A true warrior holds no excuses of why he cannot defeat his enemy and so is true with a genuine prophet of God. He is ready to take up the weapons of warfare that God has prepared for Him and to set the captive free.

Prophet of God, now is the time to face your own limitations and your own bondages and to see what has been holding you back from walking as the warrior that God has called you to be.

PROPHETIC COUNTER INSURGENCE

Book 6 of the Prophetic Field Guide Series

By Colette Toach

In "Prophetic Warrior", we learned what tools we had at our disposal in spiritual warfare, what we are facing, and how to combat it. However, it is now time to become an expert at espionage.

Learn all about the "prophetic super spy", discover strategies that can be used in spiritual warfare, receive stealth training, find the secrets to dealing with fear of the mind, and where spiritual warfare begins and ends.

A.M.I. Prophetic School

www.prophetic-school.com

Whether you are just starting out or have been along the way for some time, we all have questions.

Who better to answer them than another prophet!

With over 18 years of experience, the A.M.I. Prophetic School is the leader in the prophetic realm.

From dedicated lecturers to live streaming and graduation, the A.M.I. Prophetic School is your home away from home.

What Our Prophetic Training Accomplishes

Our extensive training is a full two-year curriculum that will:

1. Identify and confirm your prophetic call
2. Effectively train you to flow in all the gifts of the Spirit
3. Fulfill your purpose as a prophet in the local church
4. Take your hand through the prophetic training process
5. Specialist training in spiritual warfare
6. Arm you for intercession and decree
7. Minister in praise and worship
8. Achieve prophetic maturity

Contact Information

To check out our wide selection of materials, go to: www.ami-bookshop.com

Do you have any questions about any products?

Contact us at: +1 (760) 466 - 7679
(9am to 5pm California Time, Weekdays Only)

E-mail Address: admin@ami-bookshop.com

Postal Address:

>A.M.I.
>5663 Balboa Ave #416
>San Diego, CA 92111, USA

Facebook Page:
http://www.facebook.com/ApostolicMovementInternational

YouTube Page:
https://www.youtube.com/c/ApostolicMovementInternational

Twitter Page: https://twitter.com/apmoveint

Amazon.com Page: www.amazon.com/author/colettetoach

AMI Bookshop – It's not Just Knowledge, It's **Living Knowledge**

www.ingramcontent.com/pod-product-compliance
Lightning Source LLC
Chambersburg PA
CBHW072003150426
43194CB00008B/981